D0725436

THE COMPLETE
SINGER-SONGWRITER

DISCARDED
From the Nashville Public Library

THE COMPLETE
SINGER-SONGWRITER

A Troubadour's Guide to Writing, Performing, Recording, and Business

SECOND EDITION

JEFFREY PEPPER RODGERS

Backbeat Books

AN IMPRINT OF HAL LEONARD CORPORATION

Copyright © 2016 by Jeffrey Pepper Rodgers

All rights reserved. No part of this book may be reproduced in any form, without written permission, except by a newspaper or magazine reviewer who wishes to quote brief passages in connection with a review.

Published in 2016 by Backbeat Books
An Imprint of Hal Leonard Corporation
7777 West Bluemound Road
Milwaukee, WI 53213

Trade Book Division Editorial Offices
33 Plymouth St., Montclair, NJ 07042

Printed in the United States of America

Quoted lyrics by Jeffrey Pepper Rodgers © Jeffrey Pepper Rodgers Music/ASCAP, used by permission.

Excerpts and quotations from articles originally published in *Acoustic Guitar* magazine between 1990 and 2000 are reprinted by permission of Stringletter, 501 Canal Blvd., Suite J, Richmond, CA 94804-3505; acousticguitar.com.

Book Design by Lynn Bergesen

Library of Congress Cataloging-in-Publication Data is available upon request.

ISBN 978-1-4950-1991-3

www.backbeatbooks.com

CONTENTS

FOREWORD

So you want to be a songwriter! And not the writing alone at home into the wee hours, sipping wine, dreaming by yourself kind. A real touring, playing, recording, published songwriter. Like Dylan. But your own version. That's you. That's why you're holding this book.

And you're holding a good one. *The Complete Singer-Songwriter* is a guidebook that will focus you on your craft and career. And it's a great source of inspiration! Not just because it has useful business information and thought-provoking anecdotes, but also because it shows the hows and whys of a sustainable working life as a songwriter. And like songwriting itself, the business end has to be driven by inspiration.

I've been writing songs and touring for over twenty-five years, and it's an incredible way to spend your life on the planet. But we are a tribe of oddballs. Traveling, performing, creating. Walking the path of our heroes. And there's no school for this profession. It's a trial by fire. Hurdles are everywhere. Doubters are looming in the bushes. Then there's self-doubt. Financial issues. "How do I get through this?" You've probably already been accosted by the naysayers. The well-meaning doubters who ask, "No, really, what do you *do* for a living, ya' know? Like, to make *money*?" And, sometimes, they're your parents! This book is an oasis from that.

Jeffrey Pepper Rodgers takes you through all of it—from the fun stuff to the daily grind, from writing to stepping onstage and building a business around you. He schools you on the mechanics of songwriting. Informs you about some key business contracts. And the insightful quotes from working songwriters give you a true sense of belonging. Jeffrey brings you into the mindset and lifestyle of the touring professional songwriter.

If you've been an active songwriter for a while, by now you also know some of the downsides. Rejection. The difficulty of building a business that gives you enough to survive. Booking shows, keeping up with social media, finding an audience. It's enough to make Van Gogh go after the other ear. But you also know the rewards of creating and sharing your own music and becoming part of a music community.

For the great parts and the not-so-great parts of being a singer-songwriter, keep this book by your bedside—you'll need it.

Welcome to the tribe.

Ellis Paul

Ellis Paul has been a touring musician for over twenty-five years, performing over 5,000 shows. He has been the recipient of fifteen Boston Music Awards and an honorary Ph.D. from the University of Maine and has been inducted in the Maine Music Hall of Fame. His songs have been featured in numerous films and television programs and have been covered by artists in a variety of genres. He lives in Charlottesville, Virginia, when not on a highway traveling somewhere.

INTRODUCTION

One of the powerful and beautiful things about music is that it leaves you a way to express a set of emotions that has never been expressed before. Whether or not it is earth shattering or necessary even, it's just unique, and it's something the world doesn't have.

—KELLY JOE PHELPS

It might come from one little moment on a track, remixed and reimagined in your head as you walk down the street. Or from a conversation overheard in a café, or the rhythm of the windshield wipers and the summer rain. Maybe it's the way your fingers happen to fall on your instrument, suggesting a groove and a snippet of melody. Wherever it comes from, a song idea is an extraordinary yet everyday gift, and following it through to a complete expression of words and music—and then sharing the result with others—is the most creatively exhilarating experience I know.

No wonder, then, that so many people become hooked and want to make writing and performing songs an active part of their lives. Songwriting engages so many of your faculties, from the most intuitive/creative to the most analytical/practical, and that's true whether you have professional aspirations or just want to make music in the available time around your day job. One of the great things about being a musician today is that you can participate on so many levels. Even if you're not heading out on a cross-country tour, you can audition your songs at a local coffeehouse or open mic—and that may actually turn out to be the first small step toward that dream tour. The major labels may not break into a bidding war for your first album, but you can just release it yourself—even if your audience consists of only friends and family. And no matter what kind of career you choose, you can keep raising the bar on your art.

This book is written for both active and aspiring singer-songwriters, amateur and pro and all points in between, as a guide and companion for the journey from idea to song to the stage and studio and beyond. The advice and perspective in these pages is informed by my thirty-five years of writing, performing, and recording songs and my twenty-five years of interviewing singer-songwriters—legends as well as hardworking underground talents—about their careers and creative processes. Pearls of advice from these conversations appear throughout this book, along with tips and insights generously shared by producers, managers, agents, publicists, lawyers, record-company owners, and others in the singer-songwriter trade.

The opening chapters talk in detail about the songwriting process, from finding ideas to editing to collaborating, but they do *not* tell you how to write a hit song (there's a whole shelf of books for sale purporting to share the "secrets" of commercial songwriting). The philosophy of songwriting here is that if you do what you love, and pursue it passionately and relentlessly, the rest will follow. The ensuing chapters then proceed to lay out exactly what does follow, from performing and recording to promoting your music in a crowded marketplace. More and more singer-songwriters, both well-known and obscure, oversee every aspect of their music down to the last design detail of the album cover, so this book offers many tips for do-it-yourselfers. It is by no means a complete business and legal guide, but these pages are packed with real-world advice and lessons learned the hard way.

As a singer-songwriter, you wear many hats: composer, lyricist, vocalist, instrumentalist, frontman/woman, and often manager, agent, label executive, producer, publicist—not to mention roadie. No one is born with the ability to perform all these roles well, and that's the greatest challenge of this gig as well as its greatest reward. I hope this book inspires and supports you along the way.

THE COMPLETE SINGER-SONGWRITER ONLINE

Be sure to visit this book's online companion at completesingersongwriter. com, where you'll find additional songwriting lessons and tips, playlists of songs discussed in these pages, and Songwriting Tools: a selective, continually updated guide to websites, publications, organizations, and other recommended resources for songwriters.

THE FIRST VERSE

I can't say I'm the most disciplined writer. It's probably like anyone writes a song—where you might know two chords, but every time you pick up your guitar you hum this little melody because you can't play anything else. And that's how I started: I was just trying to learn how to play the guitar, but I couldn't play any songs because I didn't know how to play, so I'd kind of make up my own tunes. I never really played along with records, and I never played with other guys because they were guys and I was far too shy to pull out my guitar and play barre chords.

—Chrissie Hynde

If you can sing a song, you can write one. Chances are, you wrote one long before you realized what you were doing. As young kids, we instinctively and effortlessly play with sounds and rhythm—riffing off of a favorite nursery rhyme, rewriting "Twinkle, Twinkle," banging on pots and pans with a wooden spoon. Back when my son was a year-and-a-half old, I was pushing him on the swing while he leaned back into the sunlight. "My . . . up in the sky," he started singing, almost in a whisper—my was his word for *I* or *me* at the time. "My . . . up in the sky," over and over. His one-line song was a perfect encapsulation of that moment, and the kind of thing that's available to us all if we remain open to the sounds and emotions inside and around us.

For me, kids have been a welcome reminder that songwriting doesn't have to be a high-minded or ambitious endeavor. Some songs are just meant to be sung and forgotten on a sunny afternoon. The beauty of those blue-sky songs is that they are not a product of songwriting per se. They just appear. My son was way too young to have any notion of what he was doing or why he was doing it, so the music just flowed.

The same could be said of Chrissie Hynde, sitting in her room grappling with her first guitar chords. She started writing not because she wanted to be a songwriter, but so she would have *something* to play. Never mind if her first songs were good or bad or primitive or derivative; what matters is that she found a way into the world of songwriting. She discovered, in an entirely unintentional way, that songwriters do not belong to some exclusive club; the only requirement for entry is the desire to create and the faith that you can.

Years later, I heard a similar story from the frontman and lead songwriter of Wilco.

> *I started playing guitar when I was around thirteen, and I never really learned how to play the guitar except to write songs. That was the first thing that occurred to me when I figured out a new chord. It was a lot easier for me to write songs than to learn other people's songs, even though I was inspired by other people's songs. . . . I was isolated and deluded enough, I guess, to think that when I came up with a I–IV–V chord progression, I invented it—which is, I think, the nature of songwriting. It's got to feel like the joy of discovery.*
>
> —JEFF TWEEDY

It sounds easy, doesn't it? To start writing songs, you just *start writing songs*. For some people and in some phases of life, it is that easy. But the fact is that our culture and our own conscious minds can put up big roadblocks between us and the free creation of music. Those roadblocks *seem* big, anyway, until we get out of the car, walk right up to them, and find that they are like holograms. We can poke a finger into what looks like concrete, and then drive right through.

LOVE AND THEFT

It's a known fact: Amateurs borrow, but masters steal. When someone asks me where my inspiration comes from, I tell them it comes from what

I hear and love, from other artists. In the past I have admired certain songwriters so much (Joni Mitchell and Rickie Lee Jones, to name two) that I had to ban them from my stereo. Everything I was working on would sound like warmed-over versions of their songs. My process is still influenced by what I hear and like, but now it's more like osmosis than conscious imitation. My mind pinpoints what is unique or special and files it away somewhere. . . . I am trying to create the feeling that someone else's songs give me when I listen to them.

—PATTY LARKIN

All songs are based in some fashion on the songs that came before. In writing a song, we pay tribute to music that we love, or we steer in the exact opposite direction from the music that drives us nuts. We idolize, we satirize, we copy. We fall in love with songs; we break up and wonder how we ever could have gotten into that affair. We take *everything* personally. We listen and we remember, whether we realize it or not. Melodies, grooves, tone qualities, attitudes, images—certain musical moments have something inexplicable that hooks us and doesn't let go. And when we write songs, all these stored-away moments become the tools and spare parts that shape our new creation.

When you are starting out writing songs, it's easy to lose sight of the fact that your idols forged their style from their own idols. The young Bob Dylan obsessively copied Woody Guthrie, Okie drawl and all; the Beatles started out as a cover band, and John Lennon and Paul McCartney wrote many songs while pretending to be rock 'n' roll legends like Roy Orbison and Little Richard. But what we remember about these artists are the moments when they transcended their influences and sounded confidently and completely like themselves (thus leading to many more waves of songwriters obsessively copying *them*).

Sometimes musicians don't want to come clean about the debts they owe to their predecessors, as a matter of ego or self-promotion. Our culture worships the *new*, so artists and those who market them naturally devote a lot of energy to presenting their music as the product of some kind of immaculate conception. It's new! It's different! (But not so different that you'll think it's weird!)

You'll hear musicians talk, with a tinge of pride, about being "self-taught." Well, maybe they didn't have formal lessons with a teacher, but what about all those records they wore out, the performers whose every onstage move they studied? It's OK to be perceived as having influences, but *clone* and *wannabe* and *soundalike* are the ultimate critical put-downs. And the difference between what is derivative and what is "influenced by" is very much in the eye and ear of the beholder. When the sources of inspiration are more obscure, more diverse, or more artfully disguised, the odds go up that the music will be seen as new or original.

None of this is to suggest that being original is an unworthy goal. Quite the contrary: creating something fresh and unusual brings the deepest kind of satisfaction. But keep the concept of originality in perspective. If you feel so much in the shadow of your heroes that you despair of ever seeing the light, remember that the difference between what your heroes did and what you are doing is a matter of degree. In Patty Larkin's words, it's the subtle difference between osmosis and conscious imitation. The raw material for the creative process is the same—all the songs out there floating in the ether. Everyone starts out imitating, and with time and experience we figure out how to sound less like our heroes and more like ourselves. That means lots of listening and lots of writing, and stealing *more* rather than less.

> I'm accused all the time of ripping off this song or that song. Usually it wasn't something I was directly conscious of. You can never outright deny it, though, 'cause songs do have a life of their own, and who's to say what floats in and out of your head. I think copyright laws are pretty useless when it comes to songs. They're ineffable and they all influence each other, and I think that's how it's supposed to be. All our heroes listened to stuff and were influenced by it. Song is really primal, and since the very first song I think they've all bounced off each other. Like dust is still bopping around from the original big bang.
>
> —DAN BERN

In the end, what keeps us from endlessly rehashing old songs is our human inability to make perfect copies. Our hands don't keep the beat like a metronome does—they speed up and slow down and add that mysterious but plainly audible thing called *feel*. And in writing songs, our imaginations don't just cut and paste what we hear like a computer does. Music goes into us and through us and comes out . . . different.

Plagiarism happens, and even experienced songwriters catch themselves unconsciously "writing" a song by someone else. But it's a mistake to police yourself too closely and block the flow of music. And although you may occasionally need to distance yourself from your heroes (as Patty Larkin did, banning Joni Mitchell and Rickie Lee Jones from her stereo), it's also a mistake to refrain from loving and learning other people's songs out of fear of copying them. There's nothing more educational and inspirational for a songwriter than getting inside a great song and discovering what makes it tick.

Nashville musician Tim O'Brien shed a useful light on the relationship between other people's songs and your own. He has seen this issue from all sides: he's had a long career as a singer-songwriter; his songs have been widely covered by country, folk, and pop artists; he's covered many other people's songs onstage and on record; and he's performed and recorded lots of traditional roots music. The differences between these modes of music making, he has learned, are much smaller than they appear.

Lately I've resolved the dilemma of my identity: i.e., am I a songwriter or a traditional musician? Really, I could spend all my time in either direction but could never decide what to concentrate on. Then I realized, sometime while working with Darrell Scott, that you can't help imitating even when you write something new, and conversely, you can't help but be a little bit different from what went before. Even if you do a rendition of an old song, you'll put something of yourself onto it.

—TIM O'BRIEN

For a songwriter, the revelation that you can't help but be yourself is very liberating. I always remember a comment from Peter Mulvey, who as a teenager fell under the spell of the legendary guitarist/songwriter Leo Kottke. On Mulvey's first recordings, the Kottke influence was easy to hear. But over time, it became much harder to trace, as other influences accumulated and mixed with Mulvey's own emerging musical personality.

When I was nineteen, I just wanted to be Leo Kottke. But the thing is, I don't have either the strength or the speed and never will. And also I'm not him. There's that glaring flaw, that gaping hole in the plan, that I am not, in fact, Leo Kottke.

I think all you do as an artist is you hear things that you think are cool, and you go out and you try to do them and you fail. And that failure produces your own art—hallelujah.

—PETER MULVEY

THE MYTH OF PERFECTION

I don't think it's my job to perpetuate a myth of perfection as an artist. I really liked reading Charles Bukowski and Anaïs Nin and authors who would let me see their process, let me see how they developed. Because as a young kid, I thought, "OK, this is something I can do. You don't just start out writing The Grapes of Wrath." *And so I've never wanted to look more perfect than I am in the public eye, because why would you want to alienate people from thinking they can do what you do? I think a lot of artists enjoy that gap—they like perpetuating the myth that they are sort of a special chosen race of artistically perfect, fit people. But it's not true— there are a lot of songs I've written that aren't very good, and all you can do is put out what's honest and keep going and developing with time and just focus on development more than anything.*

—JEWEL

I was initially clueless enough to think that I could write a song. I'm sure that my early songs were not very good, but I didn't know that, so I kept writing and gradually got a little better. I think it's important to actually remain inside the egg while you hone your craft. Otherwise your spirit can be crushed by realistic feedback from the outside world.

—JOHN McCRAE

Think of a favorite track by a singer-songwriter you love. Play the song in your head, and savor the sound and style. Beautiful, isn't it? So tightly written, so powerfully performed, so crisply recorded.

Now think about everything that made that moment possible.

For starters, there's all the writing and growth that had to occur before the artist could write that particular song. Every songwriter has to work through the pale imitations, the half-baked concepts, the nice-try experiments, the can't-figure-out-what-else rhymes, the lumbering melodies, to get to the good stuff. Every time you fall short of your mark, you gain invaluable knowledge and experience. You understand mistakes you won't make in the same way again. You imagine a different approach to try next time. In other words, any song you write, no matter how good or bad or ugly you think it is, serves a purpose beyond itself: it moves you along to the place where you can write your *next* song. Behind every songwriter's best work lies a long trail of lesser tunes that did their job and can be retired from the repertoire.

Songwriting aside, many other kinds of experience help to make that favorite track of yours shine. There are the gigs, which show musicians how their own assessments of their songs square against reality—where they discover, for example, that the song they were slightly embarrassed about is in fact a crowd pleaser and that their lofty piece of musical poetry doesn't quite get across. Every performing situation, whether a dream showcase or a gig from hell, teaches something about communication that artists can apply to their next gig. And the same is true of time spent in the studio. Each track recorded is an object lesson, and musicians constantly reassess their working methods in light of their past hits and misses.

Not only does that track you love reflect hours and years of playing experience, but it is shaped by technology. There were the bad takes you never heard, the flubbed notes that were edited out, the pitches that were corrected, the effects applied, and the many rounds of tweaking during the process of mixing and mastering. All these adjustments were guided not just by the musicians, but by the engineer and producer and bystanders who offered their ears and opinions—all toward the goal of hooking you right from the downbeat.

Finally, consider the way your track was packaged—the cover art, the publicity photo, the video, and so on, all designed by multiple people to grab your attention. These things may be only tangentially related to the music, yet they strongly affect our perceptions of it. The goal of marketing and packaging is to present the product as fully realized, shiny and new, confident and hip. And this means sweeping under the rug the long and often messy process that made it possible.

That song you are thinking of is still a great song, and your admiration for it shouldn't be diminished by considering all the prep work that went on behind the scenes. But don't be blinded by the bright light reflecting off that track. The sounds captured in it are just one small artifact of a long journey. And you, with your instrument and your ambitions and your songs-in-progress, are on that very same journey.

The record business encourages us to think of music making as a stop-and-start process: each new record, released at intervals of a year or two, is a leap forward, with a batch of new ideas ready for consideration and consumption. But the reality of the musician's life is one step after another, missteps and detours and backtracks as well as forward motion. The most important thing is to keep going and to keep looking ahead rather than get discouraged by the fact that you have not yet arrived at the place where you want to be. The greatest songwriters are actually the ones who *never* arrive at that mythical place of artistic satisfaction. No matter where they are or what they achieve, they always have their eyes on the horizon.

> When you love it as much as we do, you do always feel like you're just getting started. We thought we had made it when enough people showed up to fill a room at a residency. But when you are driven and you love music and that's really what's in your heart and what's pushing you forward, you always feel like you're on the precipice of something big. We still feel that way even though we've done so many things beyond our wildest dreams. We all still feel like we're on this edge—and if we ever feel complacent, if we ever feel self-congratulatory, I think one of us will set the other straight.
>
> —BRANDI CARLILE

So think of yourself as engaged in a process rather than in creating a series of final products. Consider the example of Patrick Brayer, an underground singer-songwriter who for years has been putting out self-recorded, self-released CDs called *The Secret Hits of Patrick Brayer*—at this writing, a

BRANDI CARLILE

staggering fifty-six volumes. He gets lost in the flow of new song ideas, and he sits down every day to document them. Once a new volume is finished, he moves on and rarely looks back.

I get the bliss from the writing itself. Whether it's playing the guitar or writing a song lyric, it's the same spiritual experience for me, and it is the process that gets you there. It can't be taught and it can't be learned, and every successful individual has had to find his or her own way there. That's what you're thanking the artist for when you attend the concert or actually shell out for the CD.

—PATRICK BRAYER

FACT AND FICTION

When you do music, if you're doing it right, you're constantly telling the truth or a portion of the truth. Part of a larger truth. Even when I'm telling a story in the first person that never happened to me, some part of it is the truth or I wouldn't be able to do it.

—DAVID BROMBERG

I confess, I still haven't forgiven or forgotten her. No, not a first love who left me in the lurch, but the librarian at my elementary school. I was in first grade and thoroughly jazzed about reading. At library time, I would browse the shelves and pick out some books, then bring them to the checkout desk with some trepidation, because I knew I had to pass the test: The librarian would open my selections at random, choose a couple of big words off the page, and ask me what these words meant. If I didn't know, she wouldn't let me bring the books home. She'd send me off to find alternatives that were safely within my realm of knowledge.

I often think of this woman, and her dubious philosophy of learning, when I encounter the standard advice given to generations of writers: Write what you know. That librarian's motto was essentially the same: Read what you know. In reading, don't confuse yourself with words (or, by extension, ideas) that you don't understand; in writing, stay within your own experience. A little ambiguity or a stretch of the imagination, in other words, can be a dangerous (or at least disorienting) thing.

I'm thankful that my parents didn't apply the same filter to the books that we had at home or that I borrowed from the public library, so my mind was free to ponder the mysteries of words of all sizes. Even if I didn't go to the dictionary to look up the definition of a word I didn't know, I was still on some level glimpsing its meaning from the context of the story. My sense of the possibilities of language was expanding.

Similarly, I'm glad that when I sat down to write my first song, I didn't stop myself from writing the words that came out. Seen in the light of the standard advice to "write what you know," my lyrics were absurd: I was barely a teenager, and I was writing in the first-person voice of a middle-aged father looking regretfully and melodramatically back at divorce.

I certainly wouldn't present my Opus No. 1 as being a great song. And I couldn't even tell you exactly why I was writing that particular story—my parents' marriage was intact, and I don't recall ruminating heavily on divorce and fatherhood. Most likely I was just responding to the grown-up confessional bent of the singer-songwriters of that era—the late '70s. For whatever reason, that sad little breakup song was what I wanted to write, instead of something about what it was like to be in seventh grade. And when I was done, I could say with plenty of satisfaction that I had written a song. I was a songwriter, and primed for Opus No. 2.

It is surely the case that someone who *had* experienced divorce directly could write a more convincing song about it than I did. This is why we get the advice to write what we know. There's an undeniable power to writing about things that we've felt or seen or smelled or touched or heard. The details have a certain glow of authenticity, as one of the masters of turning personal experience into song once explained to me (via, naturally, a personal anecdote).

I didn't really begin to write songs until I crossed the border into the States in 1965. I had always written poetry, mostly because I had to on assignment. But I hated poetry in school; it always seemed shallow and contrived and insincere to me. All of the great poets seemed to be playing around with sonics and linguistics, but they were so afraid to express themselves without surrounding it in poetic legalese. Whenever they got sensitive, I don't know, I just didn't buy it.

When I read the philosopher Nietzsche in the '70s, I was delighted to hear what he wrote about poetry. He basically called it a lot of phony baloney through the philosopher figure Zarathustra, who was also a poet. After he has slandered the poets to the max, this disciple says, "But Zarathustra, how can you say this of the poets? Are you not also a poet?" "Of course," he says. "How else would I know?" And then he says, "But I see a new breed of poet, a penitent of spirit; they write in their own blood."

I believe to this day that if you are writing that which you know first-hand, it'll have greater vitality than if you're writing from other people's writings or secondhand information.

—JONI MITCHELL

Ultimately, the problem with the advice "write what you know" is that it's often interpreted too narrowly. There is so much that we "know" and even "know firsthand": not just the particulars of our own lives, but what we have seen others go through, what we've empathized with, what we've talked about, and what we've contemplated in our dreams. And there are no clean lines between these levels of knowledge—we are constantly relating what is inside our own experience to what is outside. The imagination loves to mix and match and play all around the blurry lines that separate fact and fiction, and the best art comes when we let it go free.

As listeners, we can't resist wondering whether stories told by our favorite artists in song are true or not. But as countless songwriters have told me over the years, the answer is typically not so clear-cut. Good songs are both personal and universal, whether you are writing in character or directly from your own life.

If you're writing a character that you don't understand, then you shouldn't be writing that character. You're going to be identifying with a character, and you're going to be identifying with something in you. So you're trying to find a voice that's not exactly your voice, but you're writing about feelings or emotions that you think you have an insight into.

—PAUL SIMON

PAUL SIMON

Not all my songs are right out of my life experience, but most people think they are, which I take as a compliment. That means I did my job right, because I became that person, which you need to do if you're going to write anything well. And then, oddly enough, that story ends up feeling like mine. I guess it's just called writing. You have to go to that place to write about that place.

—IRIS DeMENT

In writing songs, when you don't hold yourself up to some pseudo-journalistic standard of what is "true," all kinds of possibilities open up. I once wrote a song that was sparked by a rhythm beaten out on a table and the view of a big, beautiful sycamore tree outside the window. *Sycamore* has a great rhythm and became the basis of a chorus. I started imagining someone growing up in a house next to a sycamore tree and relating stages of childhood back to that tree. The boy in my story remains forever attached to the sycamore tree, even after he's grown up and moved away and his parents have sold the house. I started writing the lyrics in third person but eventually switched it to first person—the story felt much more compelling that way. At the end of the song, I drive back to that house, with a family of my own in the car, to see the sycamore tree once again.

So, is this a true story? At the time I wrote this song ("Sycamore Tree"), I did have a sycamore outside my house, but I had only lived there a couple of years. Many of the people I met in that town had stayed very close to where they grew up and were surrounded by extended family and lifelong friends. I envied their rootedness and felt like a carpetbagger by comparison, even as I'd enjoyed exploring different parts of the country. But my parents still lived in my childhood home, so I had a taste of what it's like to relate to a particular place throughout life, and I wanted my children to have that experience too. All these feelings were somehow transferred onto the image of the sycamore tree, and they fed into a story that was not "true"—it didn't happen to me—but was nonetheless true, on a deeper level, to what I was feeling and thinking about. This is one of the magic powers of songwriting: it can express what's inside you before you're even conscious of it.

A lot of times when you're writing in first person or what you think is first person—a sort of autobiographical song—when the song is done it is pretty much fiction. And some of the songs in the voice of a character, where I thought I was telling someone else's story, actually turn out to have a lot more autobiography in them. . . . When you're writing songs that are autobiographical, you're always writing about what you know about yourself, just like if you write about a character, you're writing about what you know about that character. It's kind of a tip-of-the-iceberg deal: a lot of stuff that you don't know you're putting into songs actually gets in there.

I like what Tom Waits says about songwriting: Just because something is true doesn't mean that it's interesting. I think that's a real good thing to keep in mind. It doesn't really matter whether the story is mine or somebody I know or something I imagined. If you write a song that's autobiographical in a closed-off way, in a diary sort of way, where it's too personal, too self-involved—that song is not going to communicate to anybody. If you write a song about something that you're dealing with that lots of other people are dealing with, too, then it can jump that gap and communicate. The only thing I think really matters in a song is, does it communicate? Is there room in it for other people to bring their hearts to it? Is there room for you to come in and kick off your shoes? If there is, then it's a good song.

*—*Greg Brown

IN SEARCH OF STYLE

A distinctive style is a musician's most prized possession. It's what allows listeners to recognize an artist within just a few notes of a song that they have never heard before. Style isn't so much *what* is being expressed in a song as *how* it is being expressed: a special quality of tone, phrasing, image, melody, or groove—or a combination of elements—that distinguishes one artist from all the others who are working with the same source material. For a singer-songwriter, a style of your own has a tremendous long-term value; it helps people to know and remember you beyond whatever particular song might have first caught their attention, and it provides a natural starting point for your songwriting now and down the road.

Sounds great, but how do you find this elusive thing called style? Are you just born with it, or do you discover it through sweat and determination and luck, like some sort of buried treasure?

Certainly one aspect of developing your own style is looking outside of yourself—pushing yourself into new territory and learning new chops. But as Suzanne Vega once memorably explained, there's another way to look at style: not as what you do in your music, but as what you *don't* do.

> *I prefer short words to long ones, because I find that's the quickest way to get someone's attention. If you say, "My name is Luka / I live on the second floor," you're drawn into this picture because it's such specific, concrete information and the language is so simple. But the funny thing was that two years ago I found out that I was an asthmatic—I had never been diagnosed as having asthma. When I mentioned this to my drummer, he laughed and said he figured there was a reason why I had such short phrases. I have short words, short phrases; I don't stand around holding the note out or using any vibrato because I can't—I have no breath! So I guess it's all developed in a way that suits my style. I mean it sounds kind of pathetic, but it isn't, really: developing a style means finding out where your limits are and making the best of them.*
>
> —Suzanne Vega

So instead of imagining a treasure hunt, think of finding your own style as chipping away at a block of stone until you sculpt a face out of it. The raw material is all there in front of you; it just needs to be given shape and personality, rendered by an artistic hand. The individual style comes in your choices of what to leave out and what to emphasize, song by song by song.

I'm often impressed by singers who seem to be able to inhabit any song from any genre; they could sing a website's privacy policy and make it sound stirring and lyrical. I envy that versatility, especially when I'm trying to work up a cover of a favorite song that sounds hopelessly lame coming out of my mouth. But I also know that as a songwriter I have a different kind of asset: a body of music that is tailor-made for my voice. I slip so comfortably into my own songs precisely because in the writing process I have made an end run around my limitations—I've mined my own style. In terms of technique, that brilliant vocalist could sing circles around me even in my own tune. But the fact is that my song and I have a special bond that nobody else can have. That relationship is one of the prime attractions of being a singer-songwriter.

Even so, in writing songs, it's not always a good thing to stay comfortably within your limitations. When you are writing an original work, you are by definition stretching beyond what you or others have done before. You don't want to rehash or be entirely predictable. In short, you want to learn something when you write.

So how do you make the most of your limitations without being confined by your limitations? By constantly pushing against them, as Jerry Garcia described in a conversation just a few years before his death. The topic was actually improvising, but the same dynamic applies to writing songs; improvisation, he pointed out, is really just "fast composition."

JERRY GARCIA

If you've got a recognizable style, that's really your limitations, you know what I mean? Basically, you play what you know how to play. And then within that, sometimes in moments of great clarity, you are able to see stuff that you don't know how to play, but it's close enough to what you do know how to play that you might try for it, and sometimes you might hit it. I tend to do that more often than is probably safe, because I frequently fuck up. Sometimes it works, and if you keep on trying at it, eventually your percentages do improve; but then it just becomes new stuff that you do know how to play.

—JERRY GARCIA

In songwriting terms, that "new stuff that you do know how to play" is your new work. Each song builds on what came before but adds a few phrases and moves to the vocabulary of your style. And what Garcia said of the hits/misses percentages holds true for songwriting as well. You have to allow yourself to fail, and the more you try, the more success you will find.

COMMERCIAL CONSIDERATIONS

All this talk about songwriting process and originality and style is fine, but what about the bottom line: Will it sell?

If only there were a simple and reliable answer to that question—the jobs of A&R people, managers, publishers, artists, and everyone else in the music business would be so much more straightforward. People could choose a comfortable spot along the spectrum from commercial music on one side to "heart music" on the other, and then reap predictable rewards for the bank account and the soul.

The problem is, the marketplace is always changing, and nobody knows exactly how or why. Music-industry people hate to admit this, but commercially driven decisions about the content of music mostly come down to doggedly following last week's trends, which could just as easily turn out to be the end of something as the beginning of something. The second application of a so-called proven formula looks like, well, a formula, and so loses all its power. Music is not chemistry, and the music business is not a controlled laboratory.

That means that an idea of what sells is a very rickety foundation on which to base your music. Maybe you're right about what will sell, but if you're wrong, what are you left with? As a developing singer-songwriter, what you need more than anything is to find your own groove, to gain a confident sense of who you are musically and what you have to say. Trying to second-guess the marketplace will inevitably confuse and distract you from that process, as a legendary singer-songwriter with a rocky youth once pointed out to me.

> *My musical style developed really in a vacuum. It developed in North Carolina with a lot of time on my hands—empty, open time—and I think that's true of a lot of musicians who develop their own thing. It takes a lot of time to practice, and it takes a certain amount of alienation to want to do that instead of wanting to do social things. It means that you in some way are cut off. It's always a funny and, I think, jarring thing when you bring these things to market, when it starts to be something that happens in a public context. It's a very iffy transition for a lot of players. . . . The marketing side is taken very seriously and gets a lot of attention and a lot of interest. It's validated, and it eats your music—it eats it up.*
>
> —James Taylor

Even experienced musicians who manage a reasonable transition from private to public spheres, from personal expression to commercial product, struggle to maintain their musical sense of self as they deal with the vagaries of the marketplace. It's depressingly common for artists who have found commercial success to flounder creatively when they fall out of favor in the music industry, as just about everyone does sooner or later. Their music has been devalued in the marketplace, and they have lost sight of its value outside of what can be expressed in unit sales and dollars.

No one should go into music as a career with the starry-eyed notion that all that matters is the art, and that the business side will just take care of itself. Of course the business matters, and bad business decisions can straitjacket your creativity just as good business decisions can set your

JAMES TAYLOR

creativity free. Once you turn your music into your profession, art and business can never be completely separated.

So how is a musician supposed to operate in the marketplace without being devoured and discarded by it? Steve Seskin, who's found commercial success as a Nashville songwriter in addition to performing his own music, said the key is to build a protective wall around the creative process.

> *I have this notion that you can mix art and commerce quite well, but that you shouldn't let the commerce poison the art. I just believe that you should create whatever you create, and then figure out how to sell it after it's done. What's wrong with that? We don't have to play starving musician our whole lives.*
>
> *In Nashville, there are a lot of writers who will sit down, and on the blackboard behind them is the cut chart of who is cutting next month*

*and what kind of songs they are looking for. I'd rather sit down and write
a song with somebody that's what we feel like doing that day, and write
the best song we can write, and then try to figure out who's looking and
who we can pitch it to.*

—STEVE SESKIN

Darrell Scott, another successful Nashville songsmith with a long-running solo career, sounded a similar note when I asked if he has any idea during the writing process whether a song might be pitchable to another artist.

*If I'm thinking of that while I am writing a song, the song is probably
sucking, because the best songs are about being true to what the song
wants to be. I have no agenda whatsoever that I'm going to steer it country
or I'm going to steer it poppy. I've played in country music all my life, but
if I have a song that wants to be really bluegrass or really mountain, I just
simply go where the song wants to go. And the odd thing to me is the
songs I've had the biggest cuts on are the ones that I was totally writing
for myself. I'm still amazed that major country acts have wanted to do
those, and I just think the bottom line is they wanted to say what I said
on my own and for myself.*

—DARRELL SCOTT

When you try to write songs according to a commercial formula or targeting a particular market/star, you overlook your greatest strengths: your own identity and point of view. You risk losing touch with what James Taylor called "the source"—the reason you got into this business in the first place.

*Just play your music, and do it for the people who love it for music. In
other words, play it in public, play it in private for people who love it, go
on the road with it, play it for other musicians, and try to minimize the
extent to which you are playing it for someone's marketing scheme, to
accommodate somebody's idea of how to sell it and how to move it as
a product. That's confusing, and that's not the point. It exists for an
emotional reason and not for a commercial one, primarily.*

—JAMES TAYLOR

STARTING POINTS

It's such a subconscious thing. It's like this little song part of you fills up over time. It's like a well, and then you just put your dipper in and dip it out. When you're a songwriter, at least a songwriter like me, you have to work hard on your craft—if you hear something, you want to be able to figure out how to do it. But the songs themselves, I don't know where they come from or where they're going or why they picked me. They really are presents, and your job is to receive them and pass them on.

—GREG BROWN

Ask songwriters where their ideas come from, and they grope for the right words or image to explain the essentially inexplicable: Songs just appear out of the blue, like lightning on a sunny day. They are forever floating past us, available to anyone who's listening. They spring from interesting mistakes and lucky accidents and, of course, from private pain and emotional turmoil. They are like fish down in the dark waters, sometimes taking your bait and sometimes not. Inspiration is a mysterious thing, and oftentimes songwriters don't even want to penetrate that mystery—they fear that if they understand what is going on, they won't be able to tap into it anymore.

Inspiration may be impossible to define or control or predict, but that doesn't mean that we have to just sit around idly waiting for it. As we will explore in this chapter, there are many ways in which we can make ourselves more receptive to inspiration and quicker to recognize it when it comes.

We can tune our ears and continually open them to new sounds. We can raise the odds that the right kinds of accidents will occur. And, as Greg Brown suggested, we can hone our craft, so that we have the necessary skills to translate what we hear and bring it to life with our own vocal cords and instruments.

What we call the songwriting process isn't really one process; it's an aggregation of processes. Songs begin life in endlessly varied ways and usually go through multiple stages—some completely unconscious, some very much driven by conscious intent—on their way to completion. The process that works for one song won't necessarily apply to the next one. The best thing we can do is to be open and ready for all possibilities.

> *There are three different musical worlds that go on in my life at once. There's the dimension of songwriting that is crafting the melodies and lyrics at all times. I've got a hundred pieces of paper, scraps, hotel stationery, and then a constant work-in-progress tape. Then there's the other side of me that just writes songs in one sitting at one time—it's the straight, lightning-bolt channel. And then right in the center there's the stream of consciousness, and I'll just sit down and ramble and write five pages of garbage. For my songwriting, that's the trinity.*
>
> —BEN HARPER

> *There are many ways to generate ideas in songwriting. You could visualize it as different doors that arrive in the same hallway. It doesn't matter which doorway you go through as long as you get into the room. So a chord structure is a way to start a song, and so is a lyric, a melody, a bass line, or a repetitive riff. It doesn't really matter which one you start with as long as you start.*
>
> —RICHARD THOMPSON

When asked about songwriting, Pete Seeger liked to quote Thomas Edison's dictum that genius is 1 percent inspiration and 99 percent perspiration. It is surely true that a flash of inspiration makes all the sweat worthwhile; it's also true that all the sweat makes it possible to receive the inspiration in the first place. Let's look at both sides of this remarkable and complex process, from idea to finished song.

BEN HARPER

FISHING FOR IDEAS

Over the years, scores of singer-songwriters have shared with me the approaches and tricks that help them find new songs and break through those dreaded periods of writer's block. Here's a compendium of ideas from those conversations. Not every one will make sense to you, but you might be surprised by how well your muse responds to the right kind of coaxing.

BABBLE.   If you ever write music before words, chances are you sing nonsense phrases or just raw sounds that fit the melody and rhythm. Usually you need to get rid of these placeholders and write "real" words (we're all glad that Paul McCartney came up with "yesterday" to replace his original words, "scrambled eggs"), but pay attention to your spontaneous utterances. Sometimes they'll point you in an interesting direction, and besides, these words or sounds are beautifully matched with the music—that's why you sang them in the first place. Run your recorder and just let the sounds flow without editing or filtering. You can look back later for usable ideas or just toss out the whole thing.

> *The process for me is usually sitting down, hitting the chord, starting to throw my voice into the chord, keeping a recorder going the whole time because I get into a sort of trance where I am stumbling around in melody land. I don't know what I'm doing. I just start singing nonsense syllables, and a word will form. Later on when I finish the song, I can go back to that work tape, and nine times out of ten the vowel sounds have already started to become what ends up being the line a month later or two months later. I really believe that there's this subconscious soup that everything is formed in, where there's a greater wisdom than my pea brain can offer me.*
>
> —BETH NIELSEN CHAPMAN

> *I often feel most fulfilled by my own things when I don't know what I'm writing about at first. I just get something that I believe in enough to sing to and mumble into a Walkman, and listen back to what I'm trying to get at without deliberating words. And then you start getting an idea. It comes around to making beautiful stuff out of junk, out of nothing, something Zen-ish.*
>
> —CHRIS WHITLEY

Many of my own songs arrive like this. I happen upon a guitar groove that catches my ear . . . find myself singing the words "turn away" over it plus a bunch of gibberish . . . record myself making all those sounds and listen back . . . and eventually start thinking, "Hmm, turn away. From what?" That one phrase and the feeling of the music points me in a direction for completing the lyrics and, in this particular case, results in a song called "Turn Away" that's about moving on from struggles of the past. I never set out to write about that topic, though. I *discovered* it, which, for me, is a much better way.

For more on how to explore this kind of unconscious creativity, see "Free Writing."

LISTEN TO YOUR INSTRUMENT.   Over the years, many guitar players have described to me how they've found songs inside particular instruments. As with the nonsense words, this experience feels like it's about listening and following, rather than guiding the creation yourself.

> *In terms of writing my songs, what happens is I come up with a little guitar line or a series of guitar chords that take me . . . well, it sounds kind of new agey, but it puts me in a place. Is it night? Is it day? And I usually just write the song exactly as I see it in my head. If the song has an attitude, then I want the lyrics to have an attitude. If the song is sad, then I want the lyrics to be sad. I think at that point the responsibility is to make everything get along.*
>
> —JOHN MAYER

> *When you write a song, if you are feeling something, somehow that gets instilled. If you are able to access that emotion, that is what is going to carry to your audience. And the way to get there is to hear the music and be taken in by it—not just to see it and label it and know it, but to be surprised by it. So I think a crucial part of what guitar can offer us is to be not just an obedient sonic slave but a teacher, a way of leading us into experiencing what this sound feels like, and having it carry us away.*
>
> —DAVID WILCOX

MAKE MISTAKES.   Many guitar-playing songwriters have gotten hooked on using alternate tunings because a new tuning undercuts what they know how to play and creates an environment for weird and interesting accidents.

That's just one example of how mistakes can generate great ideas and why they are worth cultivating.

> *If you're only working off what you know, then you can't grow. It's only through error that discovery is made, and in order to discover you have to set up some sort of situation with a random element, a strange attractor, using contemporary physics terms. The more I can surprise myself, the more I'll stay in this business, and the twiddling of the notes is one way to keep the pilgrimage going. You're constantly pulling the rug out from under yourself, so you don't get a chance to settle into any kind of formula.*
>
> —JONI MITCHELL

> *I use keyboards, which I can't play to this day, as a way of defamiliarizing myself with my musical medium. We're all trying to do this in one way or another: shake yourself loose from the pattern that your fingers are used to following. That's how you come up with something that might have a unique quality. Good things do come out of throwing yourself off the cliff one way or another.*
>
> —JOHN SEBASTIAN

EAVESDROP AND OBSERVE.   If you are paying attention, everywhere you go you'll find intriguing details that can be the starting points for constructing whole stories and characters. Who would put a "Worms Eat My Garbage" bumper sticker on her car? Did that young couple in the café ever look up from their phones and talk with each other? What's the story with that sad-looking man who trims his lawn with a pair of scissors? Try writing a song from the point of view of someone you saw at the laundromat or overheard trying to impress a date. Be a detective, and take good notes: specific words and precise images.

COLLECT TITLES.   Many songwriters keep lists of potential song titles. Woody Guthrie was an avid collector. His manuscript "How to Make Up a Ballad-song" (in the Woody Guthrie Archives) describes how he spent hours thinking of song titles and had thousands of them "laid away like postal savings bonds." John Fogerty has kept a title book for his whole career, and told me about its auspicious beginnings.

I got a little plastic book, and somewhere along the way the very first thing I wrote in it was the words "Proud Mary." I had no idea what that meant, but after that, every time I had an idea, I'd write it in that book. What I discovered was, if I had a title that sounded cool, then I'd try to write a cool song that fit the cool title. That's how "Bad Moon Rising" happened. I had written that in there, and at some point later, messing around with some chords and kind of a story, as I went through what was only a few pages then, I saw the phrase. "Yeah—that's what this is about," and I went off in that direction.

—John Fogerty

A good title can give you a big head start in writing—it can suggest a mood, an attitude, a groove, a character, and much more. A title idea might just pop up in your head, or you might overhear or see it somewhere. My own songs "Stop, Drop, and Roll," "The Day After Yesterday," "My Life Doesn't Rhyme," and "Enough About You (What About Me)" all started with their title phrases coming up in conversation. With a title, your songwriting job is about fleshing out an idea rather than pulling something out of thin air.

I like it when I get a title. Then I know, this is what it is. Generally speaking, I have to say those songs tend to be more commercial, for lack of a better word. You know, Vince Gill and I wrote "It's Hard to Kiss the Lips at Night That Chew Your Ass Out All Day Long." Well, that's a big old title and it's a joke, and you know what that is. I certainly appreciate the big title that comes to me, because those songs are easy to write.

—Rodney Crowell

WRITE IN CHARACTER. When you're not feeling the urge to write about your personal life (which may in fact be a good sign of the state of your personal life!), try writing from the point of view of a character—real or imagined.

I was very tired of singing from my perspective: I feel this way, I think that. . . . I realized that is so boring, and it's so much more fun to hear a story and colors and imagery. I would step aside from what was going on in my life, singing about me me me all the time, and just [sing about] what interests me about our lives and what can happen in them and how people feel. It's so much more interesting, because I think as a witness, you take in so much more.

—Edie Brickell

SKETCHING A CHARACTER

When teaching workshops on songwriting, Ellis Paul uses an exercise that he compares to writing a character's back story for a novel. He asks students to think of a historical character and make the following list of attributes. (Afterwards, without knowing the name, the other students try to guess the identity based on the list.) As an example here, he uses Charlie Chaplin.

1. *List five things you'd find in his bedroom.*

   A black bowler hat.
   A cane with a curled handle.
   An open script at his bedside.
   An open jar of white clown makeup.
   A red violin on his bed.

2. *List five things he sees when he looks in the mirror.*

   A headful of black tousled hair.
   Just a patch of a mustache twitching beneath his nose.
   A hint of unwashed white makeup on his cheek.
   He's practicing expressions and posing with posture like a dancer.
   His pants are too big and baggy but flow with his movements.

3. *Describe the character as a color.*

   He lives in a black-and-white world.

4. *Describe the character as a nonhuman or inanimate object.*

   He walks like a penguin but holds his space like a bird of paradise when standing still.

5. *Give the character a voice—a one-sentence quote.*

   "Every movement, every expression must tell the inner workings of the character's mind."

This example, says Paul, "reveals that physical dancer side of Chaplin's personality. I would perhaps focus on that in a song—the awareness of movement, a dance in a silent picture . . . interesting opposites there. Black and white would have a presence in the song—opposites as well—when describing the word on the page of a script, perhaps a description of his clothing, or as a metaphor for his life."

You may find that writing in character leads you into emotional territory that you otherwise would have blocked off. This is how Anaïs Mitchell described writing an album of songs centered around characters and other people's voices.

I think all the songs started from a very personal place and feelings that I have, feelings that I wake up with. It was almost for me like dressing them up in other people's clothes. I felt clear to troll the depths of some stuff without feeling like I was spilling my guts or writing a confessional song. There was a freedom in these other voices that maybe I felt more able to be honest. I might have been shy had it been me that was the speaker, the narrator.

—ANAÏS MITCHELL

ANAÏS MITCHELL

GIVE YOURSELF AN ASSIGNMENT.   Even if you never liked doing homework in school, you might get a lot of productivity and pleasure from giving yourself songwriting assignments. Look at your repertoire and try to write something a little different: a song with a particular rhyme scheme, a sweet and slow one to balance all your hard-charging songs, an epic ballad based on a newspaper story, a song with an unreliable narrator, a song with only two chords, a song with no chorus . . . See "Songwriting Games" for more ideas. Challenging yourself like this gets a different part of your brain involved in the process—the part that likes doing puzzles or figuring out programming code—and can be very energizing.

JUST SING.   No matter what instrument you play, your songwriting is dependent on your instrumental ability. One surefire way to get past your technical limitations is not to play at all. Sing while you're walking or driving; motion and changing scenery always seem to be good for sparking the imagination. Improvise over a rhythm beaten out on your chest or on the dashboard, or over a drum loop. There are two big advantages to doing this: if you just sing, the odds are high that you will come up with the elusive thing called a singable melody, which sounds good just by itself; and chances are, you will write a much simpler melody than you would otherwise allow yourself to write—sitting there with your instrument, that tune would probably seem too obvious to pursue. And when you do add some kind of accompaniment, you can do so with an ear to what the melody really needs, rather than be locked into a chord progression you came up with first.

> Personally, I find it really useful to do a lot of writing in my head, particularly at the beginning of writing a song. If I'm out walking or doing the gardening or sitting on an airplane, and I can think of a tune and lyrics, I can imagine what I would be playing on the instrument but it isn't that tied down—it's still floating around a bit. Then I go to the instrument later. I find sometimes that's a freer way of writing.
>   —RICHARD THOMPSON

EXPAND YOUR INSTRUMENTAL TECHNIQUE.   New capabilities on your instrument will surely lead you to new songs. So you might explore a new style or repertoire, take some lessons or a workshop, study a songbook or video. If you are a guitar player and strum with a pick, consider learning some fingerstyle techniques, or experiment with alternate tunings. Study jazz standards or fiddle tunes. You don't have to become a hotshot shredder—the aim is just to open up new possibilities for your writing. Strong instrumental chops are not only good for songwriting but are a major (and often undervalued) asset for performing. If you play by yourself, your accompaniment is half of your sound.

> *You really are only as good a songwriter as you are a guitar player or instrumentalist. Well, what about Bob Dylan? Bob Dylan only plays three or four chords, and he made that work for himself. But there are so many musicians that come up, so many girls with great voices and great lyrics, and they play their own instruments and they haven't learned them enough. All they can do is work with four or five chords. That's why I am really lucky and eternally grateful that the order of events happened in the way they did: I learned the neck up and down, and then when it came time to sing over stuff, I had a world of stuff I could throw at my voice to sing over.*
> —JOHN MAYER

TRY A DIFFERENT INSTRUMENT. If you can really learn your way around a second instrument, more power to you. On record and onstage, playing even one or two songs on a different instrument livens up your sound considerably. But it can be fun and fruitful to try writing even on an instrument that you don't know how to play or barely know how to play. You have an enviable kind of freedom when you have no idea what you're doing, and you can use that freedom to generate ideas.

Within the stringed instrument family alone there are many options, from banjos and bouzoukis to mandolins and ukuleles, so go explore. I've written and recorded several songs on a Strumstick, an odd little three-stringed instrument with a dulcimer-style diatonic fingerboard. I've come up with some distinctive and cool-sounding parts, but the funny thing is, when I've translated them over to the guitar (my main instrument) they sound ordinary. In other words, the Strumstick is leading me to songs I would have passed by otherwise.

JOHN MAYER

Jill Sobule described how switch-hitting on drums once helped her break a case of writer's block.

> *When I would start playing my guitar, I got really bored with it. I would start going to the same chords, the same rhythms, and I think I had to put my guitar away and find a new instrument. Once I did that I came back to my guitar and it became fresh again, and I tried to work on things like new tunings, learning more—more tools to write.*
>
> —JILL SOBULE

SWITCH MEDIA. All the art forms arise from the same basic impulses, and you can take songwriting inspiration from any medium—poetry, novels, painting, sculpture, pro wrestling, anything. Since you are working with words, books are a natural place to look for ideas on how to use language and imagery and develop memorable characters.

My own life is rich enough with disaster and metaphor to write from that, but when I am reading a book, a phrase or a line or a word just sets me off and makes my mind reel. I'll write it down and think about it, and I'll go write something on my own and come back and read. I'm constantly getting sent off in different directions by somebody's writing.

                                                    —Jennifer Kimball

You may find—as Rosanne Cash did while writing songs for her Grammy-winning album *The River and the Thread*—that you can allude directly to great literature in your songs.

My antenna is up everywhere. In "Money Road," that line about what you seek is seeking you—that's from a Rumi poem. There's a line in "World of Strange Design," too: "I'm the jewel in the shade of his weeping willow tree." The jewel in the shade is from one of Shakespeare's sonnets. I just feel like if you steal from really well-known places, it's OK.

                                                    —Rosanne Cash

Several singer-songwriters have described to me how working in another medium, like the visual arts, refreshes and improves their songwriting.

I really like writing and drawing, and I get bored doing one thing too long. It's sort of like if you are a farmer and you plant the same crop every year, it depletes the soil, but if you rotate crops it puts nutrients back in the soil, so when you go back to the same crop, it makes it stronger. For me, writing is like that. If I switch from songwriting to poetry, my songwriting gets better in my absence; whereas if I do it all the time, it just burns me out—I don't get any new information that makes my song-writing better. Sometimes just doing visual art, concentrating on pure shapes for the sake of shapes, makes my melody writing better. It makes my phrasing stronger.

                                                    —Jewel

LEARN OTHER PEOPLE'S SONGS.   Most of us learn to play an instrument by looping our favorite songs over and over, and that's a great way to inspire yourself at any stage. Getting inside somebody else's song craft expands your songwriting vocabulary and your sense of possibilities. If you want to learn someone's track note for note, go for it; but I think it can be even more illuminating to rely on your ears and your hands and come up with your own rendition or to adapt a part from a different instrument so you can't reproduce it exactly. It's amazing how often songwriters come up with new songs by failing to play someone else's song accurately.

LISTEN TO NEW MUSIC.   This seems obvious, but check out artists or genres you don't know very well, that are far from your musical home base. It's almost better if you have no chance of ever sounding like whatever you're hearing; that way, you can freely steal ideas without worrying about plagiarism. Experiencing a new artist in person, rather than just on record, can give you an even clearer sense of what makes the music tick. Festivals with eclectic lineups are a perfect place to check out a wide variety of live music without committing yourself to a full performance by an act you may or may not like.

> In any genre of music other than your own, you can come across ideas that you can import into your own style. This has been happening for thousands of years—people have been cross-pollinating musical ideas, and some of the most exciting music comes from people being influenced from other cultures.
>
> It's kind of stealing, but it's not really stealing. It's important to have your own style, first of all. Once you have your own style, you can import other things into it, and it starts to sound like you. If you don't have your own style, then you become a sort of musical chameleon or a dilettante or a musical colonialist, which are less desirable things.
>
> —RICHARD THOMPSON

ARRANGE AND REARRANGE.   If the silence is deafening and you're tired of staring at a blank page, try working with existing material. Write lyrics to a favorite melody, or set some lyrics or poetry to a new melody. Or simply take a favorite song and change it a little; that's how Alynda Lee Segarra of Hurray for the Riff Raff, like many other songwriters, got started.

> When I was traveling and I first met [fiddler] Yosi Perlstein, who plays with me, we would play some old folk songs together, like "Worried Man

Blues," and he would change some of the lyrics around so that it could be not just about men—it could be about women too. He liked to play with a simple word or something to make it more universal. That really struck me. I was very new to writing songs, probably about eighteen, and I loved that idea of taking folk music and continuing the conversation, making it new, and making it something for my generation.

Sometimes I [rework an old song] just because I'm creatively blocked and I need a point to start from.

—ALYNDA LEE SEGARRA

If you hope to use your adaptation commercially and don't want to get involved with licensing, stick to public domain sources (see "Tapping into the Public Domain"). But it can still be a great exercise to rewrite a pop hit or otherwise mess around with copyrighted material for your own amusement. The process of adapting forces you to stretch outside yourself and solve problems creatively. Here's how Duncan Sheik described the process of setting poetry to music for the album *Phantom Moon*.

Usually I write music first and then words later, whenever they come to me. So it was a little bit of an adjustment, but once I got into the process it became very natural. In fact I really enjoyed it, because it becomes this kind of fascinating puzzle, how you can make a line of text work as a musical phrase, and how you can take the structure of the given text and make that work as a musical structure in terms of the whole song. It became its own little adventure each time.

—DUNCAN SHEIK

If you have trouble breaking free from one particular version of your source material (say, you're trying to write new words to "Man of Constant Sorrow" but can't get Ralph Stanley's voice out of your head), try speeding it way up or slowing it way down, transposing it to a different key or to another instrument—anything to make the familiar seem strange and new.

USE A TEMPLATE. Another way to write without starting from scratch is to take the structure of an existing song and fill it in with your own words and music. In terms of lyrics, for instance, the song can provide you with a template for the number of lines in each section, the number of syllables in each line, and where the rhymes fall.

> *Once I was sitting in the van very late at night in Spain somewhere. I suddenly got this great idea for some lyrics and I was like, oh dang, what are we going to say, pull over? But they really were good lyrics, and it was something I'd wanted to write about for a long time. So I got out my pen and my pad in the dark, and I thought, if there's any way to do this, I'm going to have to use a template. So I took "Desolation Row" by Bob Dylan, and I just wrote the song to the tune of "Desolation Row." And when I got back to England, I picked up my guitar and I wrote a completely new tune that wasn't at all like "Desolation Row" but had the exact same scan to it.*
>
> —BILLY BRAGG

You can find all sorts of interesting song templates in traditional songs. David Wax (David Wax Museum) has written many songs by working with the structures and cadences of Mexican folk songs.

> *A lot of times what I've done is I've taken a traditional song and tried to unlock the verses and the way that the lines repeat. Lyrically, it's great to have this interesting template that you won't have used previously. Any kind of new structure feels like a great tool. It can inspire the writing in a way that wouldn't have happened otherwise.*
>
> —DAVID WAX

BE GUIDED BY VOICES.   When you're working on a song, you may find it helpful to imagine listening to a voice outside yourself. Your job isn't to write, per se, but to tune your ears so you can hear clearly.

> *I just hear voices really, and I write the melodies and the lyrics that I'm hearing. Sometimes I hear humming and then the humming morphs into words. Sometimes I just hear the voice really clear, and then sometimes I play the guitar and I hear the voice singing over what I'm playing.*
>
> —VALERIE JUNE

That voice you're hearing could also be one of your favorite artists, virtually collaborating with you in your head. A while back I was playing around with a guitar groove and melody that reminded me of Steve Earle's gritty ballads, so I imagined him singing my fledgling tune and tried to hear what he was singing about. On other occasions I've done the same thing with Tom Waits, and he's led me down a back alley I wouldn't have found otherwise. Spooky? Sure, but effective—especially because I'm constitutionally incapable of sounding like these guys. In addition to imagining what a particular artist would do with your song-in-progress, you might conjure a collaboration between two artists who never could or would be in the same room together.

Elvis Costello described writing songs while imagining the voices of Johnny Cash and other artists.

> Sometimes there's a voice guiding you with a melodic line. You may never hear them sing that song. You may have no way of getting it to them—they may not be of this earth anymore. I've written a number of songs with people's voices in mind who were not around anymore. But that's an exercise in trying to move the song toward something that moved me in that singer's or songwriter's style. I may fail miserably in getting there, but it's a little way of getting the song to shape itself.
>
> —ELVIS COSTELLO

COLLABORATE (FOR REAL). Of course, there are advantages to having a flesh-and-blood collaborator, whether a full-fledged co-writer or just someone you can bounce ideas off (for more on these topics, see "Collaborating"). I have broken quite a few logjams in my own songwriting by soliciting an off-the-cuff reaction to what I was working on from someone nearby—and he or she does not have to be a musician. Sing your embryonic melody and ask, "What does it sound like this song should be about?" Or read your verses and ask, "What should happen next in this story?"

IMAGINE AN AUDIENCE. You may also find it helpful to imagine writing a song for a particular group of people.

> I don't do well trying to write in the voice of another artist. I get bummed out. It works better for me to try to imagine playing for one of my favorite

ELVIS COSTELLO

artists' audiences. I guess it's similar, but it allows me to do it my way. If the audience loves cool guitar riffs and dark humor (à la Richard Thompson), I picture them as I try to write something. Dar Williams has such a smart, attentive, progressive audience. Several times I've written songs motivated by knowing I'd be playing gigs with her. If I wrote imagining Joan Armatrading's audience, I'd feel safe writing a heart-wrenching love ballad. So I get inspired by the aesthetic of the artist, but I try to stay in my own voice.

—CATIE CURTIS

JOIN A SONGWRITING GROUP. Songwriting organizations are ubiquitous these days, and they are well worth checking out. They provide a place to get informed feedback, moral support, and performing experience, and an upcoming meeting or showcase adds a healthy bit of deadline pressure to finish that song you're working on. As mentioned above, the group might even prod your creativity with songwriting assignments. Don't be intimidated by the prospect of being judged by your peers; in my experience, songwriting groups foster cooperation rather than competition. Connecting with your local music community is beneficial in so many ways, whether you are looking for a co-writer, a bass player to play on a demo, or someone to share the bill at a coffeehouse.

CREATE A ROUTINE. In Nashville, there are staff writers who literally go to the office and write songs nine to five, forty hours a week, forty-eight weeks a year. Even if you can't imagine creating according to that kind of corporate time clock, you might benefit from developing some sort of songwriting routine: sitting down for a defined period of time and just doing it, as a writer sits down at the keyboard or a painter sits at the easel. If you passively wait for the muse to strike, said Ed Robertson of Barenaked Ladies, there are "movies to see and food to eat and places to go." A songwriting regimen removes some of the pressure that can build up during a dry spell; instead of fretting about the weather, you're honing your craft and preparing yourself for the moment when the sky finally opens.

Usually you've got to dig through a lot of terrain to get to what you're going to want to be using. I make my notes and accumulate them, and then I need to take the time putting songs together. But you know it's like a faucet; if you stop it, when it's time to turn it back on, you might not like what you get for a little while until you let it run for a bit.

—JAKOB DYLAN

I think that writers should write at times other than when they feel like it. You can inject discipline into it, but the key is not to have expectations of how much you are going to produce during that time, because songwriting is just not like hanging Sheetrock, where your boss expects you to have hung a certain amount of Sheetrock in the eight hours that you worked. Songwriting can't be judged that way. Allan Shamblin and I wrote "Don't Laugh at Me" in about four hours. Well, we got really lucky that day. We have another story song called "Cactus in a Coffee Can" that took probably a hundred hours over a six-month period to write, because it just wasn't right. So if we get together for six hours and we come up with one line that we love, that's still a good day.

—STEVE SESKIN

CUT YOURSELF SOME SLACK. Sometimes you can block the flow of ideas just by being too quick to decide the ones that come are not good enough. Most song ideas do not arrive fully and perfectly formed; they'll have some cool aspects, and others that need work. Identifying and addressing those weaknesses is what the editing process, the subject of a later chapter, is for. Having high standards is a good thing, but you also need to keep perfectionism at bay so you can just write.

I've learned you can be too self-critical. I know people who are so critical of what they do that they get writer's block. So I realized that once I lightened up on myself a little bit, I actually wrote better. There's a delicate balance between being too critical and not being critical enough, and you have to find that middle ground and then work from there.

—DON HENLEY

SONGWRITING TOOLS

You don't *need* anything to write a song, but there are tools (aside from your instrument and its accessories) that can come in very handy. Let's take a look at what you might want to have in your toolkit.

NOTEPAD. As the old adage goes, a writer is one on whom nothing is lost. Consider yourself a reporter and a scavenger, collecting every notable idea that pops up and filing away all the intriguing details observed and overheard in your daily travels. An English teacher of mine suggested visualizing a lazy Susan—you know, one of those kitchen-table trays that spins around to pass the salt and pepper—on which you place interesting notions that you don't quite know what to do with yet, so they are stowed away yet remain within easy reach.

Many writers wind up scribbling notes on scraps and napkins that eventually disappear in the cracks of the car seat or laundry machine or who knows where. A small notebook with a pen attached, or some kind of digital notepad, can help preserve these ideas in their pure and original form, rather than as how you kinda sorta remember them.

If I'm traveling in a car and I get an idea for something, unless I write it down in my little book, it's gone. All of us have had a zillion of those—oh, man, it was such a great idea! What was that idea? You never feel exactly as you felt when you had that idea. I've noticed that I'll be sitting somewhere and not have a pencil and paper or even have a guitar, and I'll think, "I'll remember this—it's obvious." It's kind of like the movie is playing in your head. It's perfect. You're feeling all the emotions, and there's a certain way you're thinking about a topic. But then the next day or even two hours later, whenever you go to try and re-create it, it evaporated. It's just gone.

—JOHN FOGERTY

RECORDER. Every songwriter needs a recorder of some sort—quick to access, simple to use, and easy to take with you. A smartphone works great for this purpose since you're likely to have it wherever you go. Your recorder is the audio equivalent of the notepad; use it to capture cool snippets of music you happen upon.

Having the iPhone or some recording device that's mobile is really important for me. I have these little ideas all the time, and I don't necessarily finish them. If you can keep them around, most likely at some point they'll get used if they're good.

—SEAN WATKINS

A recorder can also be a great tool if you've got an accompaniment idea and need to work on the vocal part. Record a few cycles through the chord progression without singing, and then listen back and improvise melodies or words over it. I often do this while driving or walking and have finished many songs this way.

When you are further along in writing a song, use a recorder to capture rough demos. Away from your instrument, listen back to what you've got to gain some perspective and figure out where you still have work to do.

These days it's simple to do multitrack recording on any computer, and for some songs it's very helpful to hear a drum part or bass line along with the chords. But don't let the recording process divert you from the more important business of writing the best song you possibly can, as the producer and engineer Malcolm Burn (Bob Dylan, Emmylou Harris, Chris Whitley) once noted.

> *I think there's something to be said for really focusing on your songwriting and not being distracted by making elaborate demos. The more time you've been doing that, the less time you spend figuring out what it is you are trying to say. Diddling around with a snare sound or something like that is not songwriting.*
>
> —MALCOLM BURN

WORD WORKS. Songwriters are wordsmiths, and your reference library (paper or digital) should contain some of the same resources that prose and poetry writers use: a dictionary, naturally, plus a thesaurus for finding alternatives to overly familiar or already used words, and a rhyming dictionary for breaking free of *moon/June* rhymes.

> *Usually when I have a song [idea], I get a feeling of how many verses I want to have, how many choruses and bridges. Then I know the length of the song, and I get a sense of how many syllables I need and where they should rhyme to make it sound musical. I have brainstorming sessions where I write down words that could fit into the song, and with those I find synonyms. I make lists of words, basically, and make sure to have*

words that rhyme. With these sheets of words and sentences, it's easier to brainstorm a finished lyric.

—José González

BEATS AND LOOPS. Drum machines and loop generators, both stand-alone boxes and software, are used by many songwriters. Starting with a rhythm and then adding chords and melody is a very different process from working the other way around in the traditional fashion, and obviously it lends itself very well to beat-oriented pop-music styles (that is, just about all styles of pop music). It's a common weakness in songs for the melody to be too closely tied to the chord progression, and improvising a melody over a drum track can be a good way to achieve stronger, more independent melodies. Likewise, chord progressions that are composed first can be busier than they need to be; starting with a drum part may lead to leaner and better accompaniment.

Erin McKeown described why she likes using the built-in rhythm loops of Apple's GarageBand for songwriting.

The reason that I reach for it instead of sitting with the instrument is that I totally write from rhythm—that's my main inspiration for writing a song. Earlier I got enough interesting [rhythmic ideas] through the acoustic guitar, but eventually that well seemed to dry for me, and GarageBand is a supply of pretty good sounding, fairly interesting, and numerous rhythmic options. It allows chance to come in as well, in that I'll just grab something from that pile of drum sounds and rhythms.

When I'm just trying to get myself started or do something that I wouldn't have thought of myself, GarageBand is kind of like the great, dumb cousin who says interesting things.

—Erin McKeown

LIVE LOOPER. Another way to play with loops in songwriting, without using programmed or prerecorded sounds, is to create them on the fly with some sort of looping pedal. Make a kick drum sound in the mic, record it with the pedal, and loop it; play a bass line over the kick-drum pulse and loop that; then add layers of chords, riffs, vocals, and whatever else. Many solo performers use loopers in order to get a bigger sound in performance, but these pedals also provide a quick way to play with grooves and get into that trancelike zone that can be so productive for songwriting.

KT Tunstall's early hit "Black Horse and a Cherry Tree," with its insistent beat and bass line, is one song written thanks to a loop pedal. You can find many more examples in the songbooks of, for instance, Keller Williams and Ed Sheeran.

> I wrote "Black Horse" while I was trying to learn how to use the pedal. Tom Waits was an early inspiration for me, and also I used to listen to a lot of James Brown. I was really envious that these songs were over a constant groove, and singer-songwriter stuff was always so reliant on constant chord movement. I really wanted to write a song over a groove that didn't change, and the pedal was obviously perfect for that.
>
> —KT TUNSTALL

Similar caveats apply to working with loops as to using a multitrack recorder. Don't get so consumed by the technology and the recorded sound that you shortchange your song craft and wind up with what Ed Robertson called "no song hidden behind fantastic production." And treat a loop as you would any other instrument part: as something to refine and revise and perhaps leave behind. No matter what tools you use, you—not your tools—have to guide the songwriting process.

FREE WRITING

Write first, think later.

For songwriting as well as any other kind of creative writing, I'm a firm believer in this simple motto. Most songs come together in two stages: the creation, when the initial inspiration takes hold; and the editing, when you identify the good stuff, cut the bad stuff, and try to improve the stuff somewhere in between. The creation stage is all about writing whatever comes out, without filtering or second-guessing yourself. The editing stage is more rational and pragmatic, as you use your craft and any tools at your disposal to make your song as good as it can be.

> *Sometimes you have to just* do. *Later maybe you go, "This was not a good song—I'm going to tear it up now," but when you're in the act of creating, you can't second-guess yourself because then you just stop the creativity.*
> —RHIANNON GIDDENS

Many songwriters find that it's relatively easy to get into the spontaneous creation mode for writing music—just play your instrument and let yourself get swept away by the sound. For lyrics, writing freely can be trickier, especially because school has taught most of us to write according to logical, preplanned outlines. But the payoff is huge for developing your ability to write words without editing or analyzing what they mean. The more words, phrases, rhymes, and images you can spill out in the creation stage, when you are caught up in the moment, the more material you will have to work with in the editing stage. Here are some techniques and games that will help you generate lyrical ideas.

KEEP A DAILY JOURNAL. It sounds paradoxical, but you can get good results by planning to be spontaneous. Christen a notebook as your journal, or use a digital notepad if you prefer, and sit down daily to write anything that comes to mind, for a short amount of time—even ten minutes is fine. Don't worry if what you write seems trivial or weird. Just write, and then put it away and go about your day.

The point is to generate material and get into the habit of opening the spigot and letting the words out. Judgments about what you wrote and whether it's worth keeping will come at a later date.

CHOOSE AN OBJECT. You may find that you need more direction than just a designated daily writing session. One great exercise, object writing, is nicely described by Berklee songwriting teacher Pat Pattison in the book *Writing Better Lyrics*. In object writing, you choose an object—sand, map, refrigerator, potato, you name it—and write for ten minutes about any sense memories you associate with it. Don't worry about composing complete sentences, and try to engage as many senses as possible: not just sight, smell, taste, feel, and sound, but organic sense (what's going on inside your body—for example, nervous jitters or fatigue) and kinesthetic sense (which Pattison describes as your sense of relation to the world around you, like seasickness or drunkenness).

One of the benefits of object writing is that on the surface you're writing about an object, not yourself, so you're less self-conscious. And yet when you do this well you reveal a lot about yourself, through your perceptions and memories.

MAKE WORD LISTS.   Wilco's Jeff Tweedy is a fan of word games. He once told me how he likes to compile lists of words as a way to bring an element of chance to the writing process—and discover strange and compelling phrases he wouldn't have thought of on his own.

> *I make lists of words I like that are all related to one topic, and set them against words that I'm just finding beautiful at the time. I love having a verb act on a word that you're not used to it acting on, and vice versa—I like having nouns made into verbs that you don't expect. Sometimes I just take all the verbs out of an Emily Dickinson poem and put them on one side of a page and take all the nouns out of a, you know, Robert Frost poem and put them on the other side of the page, and see if anything interesting happens.*
>
> —JEFF TWEEDY

Try making word lists using stylistically different books—they don't need to be poetry or even literary. (My songwriting class had fun doing this with one batch of words from a social-science textbook and the other from Tina Fey's *Bossypants*.) You can, as Tweedy said, collect nouns and verbs, or mix adjectives and nouns (a little like Mad Libs), or you can ignore the parts of speech entirely and grab any words that seem juicy. It's even better if your list includes words not normally found in songs—that will certainly steer you away from songwriting clichés.

EXQUISITE CORPSE.   For this adaptation of a classic writing game, created by French surrealists in the early 20th century, you need a group of writers—the more the merrier.

1. Each person in the group takes a sheet of lined paper and writes a single line of verse at the top. Use a stopwatch and allow no more than one minute for everyone to write. If you like, use a word list to get started: pick some words randomly from a book and use those to compose the first line.

2. Pass the paper to the writer on the left, who reads the first line, adds a second line that responds somehow to the first, and then folds the paper so that only the newest line is visible. Again, move fast so no one can deliberate—one minute or less.

3. Pass the paper to the next writer, who does the same: reads a line, adds a line, folds the paper so that only the last line is visible, and passes it again.

4. Keep going until you've filled the page, and have the last person write something that feels like an ending.

This kind of group creation, in which no single person knows where the writing has gone and where it's going, never fails to be funny—and it can come out unexpectedly deep. When each writer follows the drift of the previous line, the whole piece often seems to have a plot and dreamlike logic.

One variation on exquisite corpse is best played in a noisy and distracting environment, like a bar, in which it's impossible to concentrate. With a partner or a small group of friends, pass a sheet of paper or napkin back and forth, writing a line at a time without talking about what you're doing—you can even do this while carrying on a conversation about something else. With all the distractions there's no need to fold the paper. Again, the point is to write quickly, without thinking, and to let serendipity take charge.

WRITE YOURSELF DOWN. Here is an exercise used by Ferron in her writing workshops—another way, as she put it, to "short-circuit the judgmental mind." Get a piece of paper and pen and start writing fast—no pausing or editing—until you get to the end of the page. Then make a fist in the center of the page and draw a circle around it.

Oddly enough, the words inside that circle are usually what you want to talk about—and what you don't want to talk about. So go into it and keep writing yourself down until you've got your true voice talking, where your child and your adult and your longing and your losses all come together. We do that with good friends—we know what it sounds like when we're getting authentic.

—FERRON

LET IT REST.   However you go about free writing, don't try to do anything right away with the results. Let time pass, so you can read over the words as if they were written by someone else. That distance will help you shift into the second phase of writing, when your inner editor sits down and says, "Alright, let's see if there's anything good in here." Some of what you wrote will seem odd or pointless, but here and there you may discover the seeds of new songs.

Free writing serves as a reminder that, subconsciously, you know more than you realize at the time. I've found that I can express feelings and thoughts long before I recognize or understand them. Approached in this open-ended way, writing becomes a process of discovering what you want to write about. So let go of the steering wheel and see where you end up.

SONGWRITING GAMES

Every songwriter needs a nudge sometimes to keep writing. There's no better way to learn and grow creatively than by simply finishing songs, but that can be easier said than done. What do you do when inspiration is not sweeping you off your feet, and the song ideas that you come up with seem dull and hackneyed?

One approach used by many songwriting groups is to play different kinds of creative games that involve writing a song according to specific parameters, and setting a deadline. Yes, this is a form of songwriting homework, but the process of writing to spec like this can be playful and fun. It's a relief sometimes to be given direction rather than always having to find your own way, and it will lead you to very different songs than you would typically write. Here are a few types of games that can help keep the ideas and songs coming.

WORDPLAY.   The simplest songwriting game is to start with a word or phrase and write a song that incorporates it—the word or phrase doesn't have to be the title or even a central element; it just needs to appear somewhere in the lyrics. This is the game notably played by Jason Mraz and the email songwriting group led by Austin musician Bob Schneider. As Mraz told me, his hit duet "Lucky" with Colbie Caillat, for instance, started from the phrase *me talking to you* (the opening lines are "Can you hear me? I'm talking to you"). Everyone in the group takes a turn giving the prompt—which might be as simple as *brown* or as odd as the nonsense word *gumanema*.

> *It's not like a competition; it's more like a songwriter support group, where one songwriter says, "I wish the wind would blow me" and then you have to use that phrase in the song and the deadline is Tuesday at midnight. The whole idea is that you just write the song you feel inspired to write, and don't think about if it's going to be a single or if anyone is going to like it.*
>
> *I find it to be tremendously helpful. It creates this demand for more songs. A record label could certainly be asking where the next songs are, but when you have real songwriters, guys who are doing the hustle just like you, guys who want to live romantically with words and music and leave something behind, then you feel like you're in a safe place and a noble place, an honored place to write music. So it works for me. It also gives us all an opportunity to write a lot of crap and get that out of the way, because for every great song you've got to write a hundred really shitty songs.*
>
> —JASON MRAZ

It is possible to play this game solo and choose words for yourself, maybe by randomly picking words from a book or introducing another element of chance, but it's more interesting to do with a partner or group—input from others forces you out of your usual patterns of thinking.

Once I was booked for a songwriter showcase and given the task of writing/performing a song with the phrase "the shortest straw." At first I

JASON MRAZ

was flummoxed—I couldn't imagine what to do with those words. But before I even had a chance to think more about it, I found myself imagining a character who feels perennially shortchanged in life, and ad-libbing lyrics over an E minor groove. Even though "the shortest straw" is just a minor detail in the resulting song (titled "Prayer"), this assignment gave me the impetus and the deadline to finish what turned out to be a keeper.

When playing this game, I recommend using words for physical/tangible things, and it's a bonus if they have multiple uses or meanings. For instance, in my songwriting group we've used *key* and *ticket* (resulting, for me, in the songs "I've Got It Here Somewhere" and "Closer"). See "Free Writing" for more on how to generate raw material for lyrics starting from objects like these.

You can also use words that define a theme or concept but don't have to appear in the song itself—the game could be to write about envy, winter, or working in a cubicle. Avoid cliché themes (the road, breakups, Saturday night), and pick something that points the lyrics in an unexpected direction.

STORYTELLING STYLE. Another area to explore in songwriting games is the way the story is told. There are so many possibilities beyond the usual contemporary style of describing your own experiences in first person. Here are a few prompts you might use in a songwriting game:

- Write entirely in second person—not singing to you (as in "I want you") but placing *you* at the center of the action, as in the Beatles' "Lucy in the Sky with Diamonds" ("Somebody calls you, you answer quite slowly . . .").
- Write in third person (he/she), even if the story is autobiographical. Writing about your own experience in third person may help you feel free to tweak the details, like a fiction writer, in order to make a better story.
- Write in first person but make the story specifically and obviously *not* about you. Tell the story of someone from a different era, or living in a different kind of place, or older/younger than you are. Writing from the perspective of someone of the opposite sex is tricky but worth trying.
- Write in the voice of an unlikeable, unreliable, or otherwise flawed character. Two masters of this are Richard Thompson and Elvis Costello, who have brought us inside the heads of some downright scary narrators. Remember that it's essential to empathize somehow with your character, however awful he or she may be, so that the listener can connect emotionally with the story.

SAMPLE SONGWRITING GAMES

Write a song . . .

- with the word *alarm*.
- with the phrase "It's all good."
- about losing memories.
- from a child's perspective.
- narrated by an abusive spouse.
- with a nonsense title (as in "Ob-La-Di, Ob-La-Da," "Be-Bop-a-Lula").
- with the rhyme scheme (not the band) ABBA.
- in which no lines rhyme but the last line of each verse is the same.
- with the Bo Diddley rhythm.
- for a barn dance.
- with spoken verses and a sung chorus.

RHYME TIME. You can create some interesting songwriting challenges by zeroing in on the rhyme scheme. Many songs follow the patterns ABAB (in which lines one and three rhyme and lines three and four rhyme) or AABB. If you hear a song with a striking rhyme scheme, figure out what it is and use that for your songwriting game. How about trying the verse pattern of Bob Dylan's "Blowin' in the Wind," which goes XAXA (alternating unrhymed and rhymed lines)? Or Joni Mitchell's "Both Sides Now," in which the verses go AAA and the fourth line ends with the same word each time (in her case,

way)? Or how about the extended rhyme scheme of Leonard Cohen's "Hallelujah," AACBBC?

For songwriters coming out of folk, country, rock, and pop traditions, rap is a rich source of fresh rhyming ideas. For a songwriting game, you might take your cue from rappers and try writing long lines with the rhymes in the middle rather than the end.

For more about rhyme schemes, see the "Song Form" chapter.

PLAY ON. All the games described above start with lyrical prompts, but of course you can also focus on the music. The game can be to write in a genre like bluegrass or reggae, though you need to be wary of falling into genre clichés. You can focus on the time signature and write, say, a country waltz or a song with a fast 6/8 rhythm. Or you can base the game on song structure: as a change-up from the old verse/chorus, try writing a song in a traditional ballad form with only verses, or a song with an instrumental bridge. Coming up with the game rules is a fun, creative game in itself.

Look at a songwriting game as a chance to do something you don't normally do. Get outside your comfort zone, stretch your capabilities, and don't be too critical of the results. Let yourself write songs that are goofy or weird or that you may never play in public—you will learn as much, or more, from failed experiments as from your best efforts. The important thing is that you're writing, and whenever inspiration does strike, you'll be ready.

SONG FORM

You start writing a song because you feel something—there's an image or phrase or sound you want to explore further. Ideally that original inspiration shapes every aspect of the song, from the melody and chord progression to the rhythmic feel, the lyrical style, and the structure of the verses and chorus. As you write, your song takes on an identifiable form and a set of patterns, but you don't begin the process by choosing a form; that would be like deciding to write a novel that has a dozen twenty-five-page chapters and an epilogue . . . before coming up with a story idea. To paraphrase e. e. cummings, the feeling is first, so you don't pay attention to syntax—you follow the feeling.

Once you are past the initial stages and are in the middle of working on a song, however, it is useful to start paying attention to syntax. The small ideas you started with—a string of chords, a snippet of melody, a few lines of lyrics—begin to suggest an architecture for the whole song, and identifying that structure helps you figure out how to complete the building so that it's strong and coherent.

In this chapter we will look at some of the structural ideas that are particularly important for songwriting: the form of the song and the patterns of rhyme. You can hear many of the songs mentioned on the companion playlists at completesingersongwriter.com.

PARTS OF A SONG

Beneath all the nuances of melodies and lyrics, most songs are built from the same basic parts—some kind of sequence of verse, chorus, bridge, and so on. For writing a song, learning to play someone else's song, or communicating with other musicians, being able to identify these parts and patterns is an essential skill.

Let's take a look at some common song forms used in rock, country, folk, and pop, and consider how their components function and fit together.

VERSE ONLY. The simplest song form has only one section, the verse—the same melody and chord progression repeats through the entire thing while the words change. This is the traditional ballad form, as used for instance in "Pretty Polly," "The House Carpenter," and "Man of Constant Sorrow," and carried on by such songwriters as Bob Dylan ("All Along the Watchtower"), Chuck Berry ("Promised Land"), and Richard Thompson ("1952 Vincent Black Lightning").

As these examples suggest, the verse-only form is a great storytelling vehicle (murder and tragedy are optional but recommended). Since the music isn't changing, listeners can focus on the unfolding narrative. So you might consider writing in this form when the story is the most important aspect of the song.

VERSE WITH REFRAIN. Some songs use the verse-only form, but each verse ends (or sometimes begins) with the same phrase or line—the refrain. The refrain usually contains the song's title too. Examples include Johnny Cash's "I Walk the Line," Dylan's "The Times They Are A-Changin'," Paul Simon's "Bridge Over Troubled Water," and Wilco/Woody Guthrie's "California Stars."

The line can be a little blurry between a refrain and a chorus (covered next). The difference is that a refrain is shorter—usually just one line of lyrics—and doesn't feel like a separate section of the song. It's more like the conclusion of the verse.

The verse-refrain form retains the storytelling power of using verses only, while adding the benefits of repetition for sticking in a listener's memory.

VERSE AND CHORUS.   You know the chorus when it hits: it's the sing-along and raise-your-lighter part, with the same words each time and almost always the song's hook/title, in a distinct section that repeats typically three or four times. While the verses carry the story forward, the chorus nails the song's main theme, image, or feeling.

The simplest type of chorus uses the same music as the verse, as in "This Land Is Your Land," "Will the Circle Be Unbroken," and "You Are My Sunshine." Usually, though, the chorus brings a change of melody—often rising into a higher register. Examples of verse-chorus songs with a contrasting chorus include Stephen Foster's "Oh! Susannah," James Taylor's "Sweet Baby James," the Eagles' "Peaceful Easy Feeling," and Bob Dylan/Old Crow Medicine Show's "Wagon Wheel." Beck's "Loser" follows a pattern that you'll hear pretty much anytime you turn on pop radio nowadays: rapped verses and a sung chorus.

It's tougher to tell a complex story in a verse-chorus song, simply because the repeating chorus takes up much of the space. Instead, the strength of the verse-chorus form is capturing a feeling . . . and then lodging in listeners' heads.

VERSE AND BRIDGE.   Some songs have a second contrasting section, with a different melody and chords than the verse, that doesn't feel like the focal point of the song the way a chorus does. It's more like a short diversion from the verses, and it's not repeated over and over—it comes up once or maybe twice. That contrasting section is the bridge, also known (especially on the eastern side of the Atlantic) as the middle eight.

Songs that use only a verse and bridge often have an old-fashioned sound, because the 32-bar AABA form was standard in Tin Pan Alley songwriting. Examples include Harold Arlen and Yip Harburg's "Over the Rainbow" (the bridge begins, "One day I wish upon a star"), Paul McCartney's "Yesterday" ("Why she had to go"), and John Lennon's "Imagine" ("You may say I'm a dreamer").

In terms of the music, the bridge often modulates to a new key, changes up the rhythmic feel, or introduces a melodic idea quite different from the verse.

VERSE, CHORUS, AND BRIDGE.   Using a three-part form of verse, chorus, and bridge opens up a lot of possibilities for songwriting. With three parts, the verses move the story along, the chorus delivers the hook, and the bridge gives listeners a break from the predictable back and forth of verse/chorus. Many songs use a structure like verse-chorus/verse-chorus/bridge/verse-chorus, where the bridge provides a refreshing change before the final verse and chorus.

The Lennon and McCartney catalogue is chock full of clever uses of the verse-chorus-bridge (I mean middle eight) form. For instance, "I Want to Hold Your Hand" follows the verse-chorus/verse-chorus/bridge/verse-chorus form mentioned above and then adds on one more bridge/verse-chorus (the bridge is, "And when I touch you . . ."). "Eight Days a Week" uses the exact same form (with the addition of an intro and outro—more on those below), as does "Ob-La-Di, Ob-La-Da."

PRECHORUS.   Especially in the realm of pop/rock, songwriters often write a prechorus, a short section of four bars or so that sets up the chorus and uses the same words/music each time. Think of Tom Petty's "Refugee"; the prechorus goes: "It don't make no difference to me . . ." and builds anticipation for the chorus: "You don't have to live like a refugee." Similarly, in Creedence Clearwater Revival's "Proud Mary," the prechorus starts with "Big wheels keep on turning" and leads into the chorus: "Rolling on the river."

To pick a few examples off the more recent pop charts, Daft Punk's "Get Lucky" has a prechorus beginning with "We've come so far," and Lorde's "Royals" has an extended prechorus starting with "But every song's like gold teeth, Grey Goose, trippin' in the bathroom." In both cases, these repeating sections launch into the big chorus and, you guessed it, the title/hook.

Many pop songs skip the bridge and just use a verse-prechorus-chorus form. The prechorus-chorus combo maximizes repetition . . . and makes it so the song is hard to get out of your head even when you dearly wish you could.

INTROS, OUTROS, AND INTERLUDES.   In addition to the major sections above, a song may have smaller bits and pieces that add a little variety. At the top might be an intro, which is typically a short instrumental passage—sometimes built from a piece of the chorus or another part of the song. At the end, a song may have an outro (also known, more formally, as a coda). The outro is sometimes an extension of the last chorus, with some kind of development in the melody, harmony, or words.

To cite some songs mentioned above: "Over the Rainbow" has a coda with the line "If happy little bluebirds fly beyond the rainbow, why oh why can't I?" And "Eight Days a Week" uses the same up-the-neck guitar riff for its instrumental intro and outro.

In the middle of songs, too, there are often interludes that provide a little breathing room—for instance, between the chorus and the next verse or the bridge. Most commonly an interlude simply repeats the intro. That's what happens in "Proud Mary," where the intro chord pattern returns as an interlude after the chorus a couple of times.

USING SONG FORM.   These basic components of songs may be familiar to you, but you can learn a lot by paying closer attention to them. When you listen to songs, try identifying the sections. Oftentimes you'll be able to guess what's next—for instance, after a verse/chorus, verse/chorus, there's a good bet a bridge or interlude is coming. It's also illuminating to notice when songwriters arrange the parts in an unexpected way—you can find structural ideas to try in your own songwriting.

Becoming more conversant with song form gives you an easy shorthand for communicating with other musicians. And in writing, a good sense of structure can provide you with a kind of schematic for a song in progress— that'll help you figure out how many verses you need, or if the song is too repetitive and could really use a bridge. Now your job is to fill in these sections with the story that wants to be told.

USING RHYME

Songs don't have to rhyme, as demonstrated by unrhyming classics such as Paul Simon's "America," John Lennon's "Across the Universe," Suzanne Vega's

"Tom's Diner," and Sting's "Fields of Gold." Yet most songs do rhyme, and for good reason. A rhyme helps lyrics lodge into people's heads, focuses their attention on key words and phrases, and solidifies the structure of a song—a rhyme pattern clearly outlines a verse or chorus, for instance. Good rhyming adds rhythm and zing to the words.

No wonder, then, that rhyme is a bit of an obsession among songwriters. Rhyming is such a natural thing, instilled in us since our days of Mother Goose and *The Cat in the Hat*, yet it's notoriously difficult to do well— especially since rhyming words have been so thoroughly picked over by songwriters and poets over the ages. How do you use rhyme effectively without sounding trite, turning to worn-out rhymes like *chance/dance/ romance*, or resorting to *unfurled* just because you needed a rhyme with *world*? As with chord progressions, melody, and other aspects of songwriting, the key is developing a good, flexible vocabulary. That's what we'll explore in this section.

RHYME SCHEMES.   The most traditional and familiar rhymes fall at the end of a line, and they follow a rhyme scheme or pattern that usually repeats within the same section throughout the song. Here are some common rhyme schemes, with examples drawn from my own songs.

AABB.   Many songs use couplets—the lines rhyme in pairs. "My Life Doesn't Rhyme," a song about songwriting, opens with three couplets.

> *Searching for chords that'll turn like a wheel [A]*
> *As I try to interpret the way that I feel [A]*
> *Wishing for words that'll glimmer like pearls [B]*
> *No, I never stop hoping to impress all the girls [B]*
> *Too ancient for* Idol, *too young to expire [C]*
> *Here's why this songwriter does not retire [C]*

AAAB.   You can also use rhyme in groups of three (or even four, though that can get old fast). In the story song "Sycamore Tree," each verse has a triplet rhyme, and then the last line ends with the title phrase.

> *The grass tickles on my feet [A]*
> *When I'm rocking in my bouncy seat [A]*

> *The summer breezes smell so sweet [A]*
> *Blowing by the sycamore tree [B]*

ABAB.   With this pattern the rhymes interlock, creating a tight four-line unit. From "Somehow":

> *I want your hair on my shoulder [A]*
> *I want to breathe you now [B]*
> *Feeling our hands getting bolder [A]*
> *Somehow somehow [B]*

You can combine couplets and interlocking rhymes to create longer patterns, like this one, from "The Day After Yesterday." (Note that in the fourth line the rhyming word, track, isn't actually the last word of the line, adding a little irregularity to the pattern.)

> *The day after yesterday I lost my luck [A]*
> *Sped right off in an old milk truck [A]*
> *Oh I heard it clinking away [B]*
> *The sky was yellow and the sun was black [C]*
> *Rise or set—I can't keep track sometimes [C]*
> *It's been a very big day [B]*

ABBA.   Much less common in songs than AABB or ABAB rhyme schemes, ABBA can be an interesting choice. The bridge of "My Life Doesn't Rhyme" uses this pattern (after a first line, marked with an "X," that doesn't rhyme with anything):

> *Heartache and quiet desperation [X]*
> *Are a songwriter's very best friend [A]*
> *But a song with a rhyme [B]*
> *And a good sense of time [B]*
> *Will carry you through to the end [A]*

USING UNRHYMED LINES.   As the last example suggests, you don't need to rhyme every line. Mixing rhymed and unrhymed lines makes the lyrics less predictable and tidy. You could, for instance, rhyme two of the four lines in a stanza, using the rhyme schemes AXAX, AXXA, or XAXA, where "X" again represents an unrhyming line. From "American Dream":

When you're out on the road [X]
Driving alone [A]
With the rising moon [X]
A sliver of bone [A]

VARYING THE RHYME SCHEMES.   Rhyme schemes can help build contrast between the sections of a song. If the verses are ABAB, you might switch to AABB on the chorus, for instance, and then use no rhymes at all on the bridge. These changes in the rhyme scheme should go hand in hand, of course, with the other changes in the melody, the length and phrasing of lines, the chord progression, and so on. Think of all these aspects of the song as reinforcing each other to create the total effect you want.

PERFECT RHYMES (AND THEIR PITFALLS).   All of the lyric examples given above use perfect rhymes—the rhyming words end with the same accented vowel/consonant sound. A perfect rhyme is satisfying for sure, especially when it's unusual (I confess to deriving a lot of songwriterly pleasure from rhyming *tryin'* with *online* in the song "Eight Days in January"). For some songwriters, coming more from the Tin Pan Alley school, perfect rhymes are the *only* acceptable rhymes. If you can stick with perfect rhymes while keeping the words fresh and saying what you want to say, well done. But beware of fixating on perfect rhymes.

> **MAPPING OUT RHYMES**
>
> If (like me) you are not conscious while you write of the rhyme patterns you're using, it's an interesting exercise to go through your catalogue of songs and map out the rhyme schemes. You may well discover that you use just a few rhyme schemes over and over. Map out some of your favorite songs by others, too, to see how their rhyme schemes compare with yours.
>
> Now try putting this information to use. If you've got lyrics in progress that you're not satisfied with, see if you can alter them to fit a different rhyme scheme. Just focus on the words at first without worrying about the music; once you have the words working on the page, you can turn your attention to adapting the melody and phrasing.

Rhyme is a trap sometimes just because obviously if you're trying to make the end of every line rhyme, that limits your lyrical content and can dumb it down. When you're doing a rhyme pattern, a listener can almost guess what the next line is going to end with. So if you can get away from

using a rhyme, you can have a more interesting approach to your lyrics and keep people guessing, which is kind of the magic of songwriting.
—G. LOVE

In comic or novelty songs, rhymes that are a little ridiculous can make the song funnier (as in "Atheists Don't Have No Songs," where Steve Martin rhymes "a Bach cantata" with a line about how atheists' songs "add up to nada"), and in rap, proving your rhyming dexterity is part of the game. In these contexts, putting rhymes in the spotlight makes sense. But in other types of songs, good rhymes are more in the background, quietly serving the song. Rhymes that draw attention to themselves can take listeners out of the story and emotion of the song—the songwriter's craft (or lack thereof) becomes the focus.

As you work on lyrics, be alert for when you're forcing a rhyme, by stressing a normally unstressed syllable of a word (for instance, saying "no-*thing*" to rhyme with "*sing*") or using convoluted syntax (saying "So much in love with me you'd fall" in order to rhyme *fall* with the previous line). Ideally, lyrics flow in the same way they would if spoken. They sound natural and, hey, they rhyme too.

One caveat, though, on the topic of forced rhymes. I can't help but think of Bob Dylan rhyming *knowed* with *road* in "Don't Think Twice, It's All Right," or Leonard Cohen using the slangy pronunciations "do ya," "overthrew ya," and so on to rhyme with the title of "Hallelujah." On paper, these rhymes look bad—if these songs were unknown and brought to a songwriting workshop, no doubt some people would tell Leonard and Bob that their songs needed more work. In truth, if all songs with sloppy and forced rhymes were removed from the airwaves, many radio stations would go mostly silent. The point being, rhyme is just one factor in what makes a song successful—however you define success. With rhyme as well as all other aspects of songwriting, you tune your ear to what you like, and you set your own bar.

NEAR RHYMES. One way to go beyond the limited choices of perfect rhyme is to use words that sort of rhyme—they are referred to variously as near rhymes, slant rhymes, half rhymes, or just imperfect rhymes. Near rhymes are all over the place in contemporary songwriting: *down/around, home/ phone, sleep/street, spin/again, road/side, love/move*, and so on. If you open your lyrical vocabulary to near rhymes, you've got way more options; though you lose some of the ring of a perfect rhyme, you can gain by having access to less common and potentially more interesting words. Near rhymes can also allow you to rhyme the seemingly unrhymable (even *orange*, as Eminem famously demonstrated in a *60 Minutes* interview by freestyling "I put my orange four-inch door hinge in storage and ate porridge with George").

With near rhymes, you use either the same vowel sound and different consonant (*line/time, phrase/trade*), or a different vowel sound and the same consonant (*hot/doubt, friend/stand*).

INTERNAL RHYME. You can spice up the rhyming in a song by using rhymes in the middle rather than at the end of the line. Rap lyrics use tons of internal rhymes (as in Eminem's *orange* example). James Taylor drops them throughout "Let It All Fall Down": "Sing a song for the wrong and the wicked and the strong / And the sick as thick as thieves."

Although it's not rhyme, strictly speaking, a related technique for making lines of lyrics hang together is alliteration, or repeating consonant sounds at the beginnings of words. The JT lyrics just quoted have quite a bit of alliteration (*s* and *th* sounds). Another example is this great, twisted line from Warren Zevon's "Werewolves of London": "Little old lady got mutilated late last night," which is jam-packed with *l* sounds.

The first line in this stanza from my song "Humming My Way Back Home" goes heavy on alliteration with the *l* sound, and the last line uses internal near rhymes: *give/love/we've*.

> *Living is longings and lessons half-learned*
> *Our words tangle up in a knot*
> *Let's forget what we've given, forget what we've earned*
> *Give thanks for the love that we've got*

STRATEGIES FOR FINDING RHYMES. Sometimes rhymes just fall into place when you're writing lyrics, but in many cases it takes work to find them. Making lists of potential rhymes can really help. You can generate them in your head: if you need to rhyme with *done*, for instance, just run through the alphabet for the preceding consonant to find *bun*, *fun*, *gun*, *none*, and so on. Be sure to consider consonant combinations, too, that give you *spun*, *shun*, *stun*, and more, as well as two-syllable or longer words such as *begun* and *outrun*. And then you can extend your search to near rhymes: *hum*, *trunk*, *front*, *crunch*, *overcome*.

You can get help with this process by using a rhyming dictionary. Some will give you not only perfect rhymes but near rhymes. If you want to take a more analytical approach, there are also books that dig deeply into the mechanics of rhyme and related topics such as meter and stresses. (See completesingersongwriter.com for recommendations of rhyming resources.)

As you compile a list of possible rhymes, look for words that not only rhyme and sing well but match what Dar Williams called the song's voice—encompassing its musical, emotional, and narrative voice. She

DAR WILLIAMS

gave this example based on looking for an end rhyme for the line "It's not my fault."

> *Every song has a voice, and you have to decide on word rhymes based on the voice. Is it a medieval voice, is it a modern voice, is it an anxious voice? I go through the list of options based on the voice of the song. I'll riddle it through for a while, but if nothing works, then I have to change the word* fault. *It's just that simple.*
>
> *When it's going well, that's really fun. You have* vault, *and sometimes you'll discover that* vault *is exactly the word—and then suddenly you have this whole metaphor of currency and secrecy or something that you realize would be perfect for the song. So rhymes can give you serendipity.*
>
> —DAR WILLIAMS

Ultimately, rhymes and rhyme schemes are a secondary consideration in songwriting; they are the tail and should not wag the dog. So let your idea guide you. Just start singing and tune your ear for which lines seem to want rhymes. Often you can tell where the rhymes should fall, and even what vowel sounds work well, when you're still singing nonsense sounds.

Once you've arrived at a pattern for each section, try to maintain it through the whole song, but make sure you don't sacrifice the voice, meaning, or natural flow of the language in order to land a rhyme. An irregularity in the rhyme pattern here and there will be forgiven, forgotten, or not noticed at all by listeners—in fact, an unpredictable moment may serve to hold their attention.

UNDERSTANDING CHORD PROGRESSIONS

Chord progressions are the engine of songwriting. The melodic or lyrical hook may be what lodges in people's heads, and an insistent beat may dominate the mix, but the chord progression is what makes everything *move*. By itself, a chord is just a static thing—a few notes stacked together—but a group of chords arranged artfully in a progression creates a little harmonic journey. There's a kind of magic in a great chord progression, a mix of soothing familiarity and thrilling surprise that has emotional power even without the melody and lyrics.

So every songwriter needs to be fluent with chord progressions, but the process of figuring out which chords to use and how to sequence them can be mystifying. You can create progressions by randomly trying chords, but with a basic theoretical understanding of chords and keys, you can zero in much more quickly on good options to try in a progression—and become a more productive and versatile songwriter overall.

In this chapter, we'll take a look under the hood of some popular songs and explore how chord progressions work. We'll build a vocabulary of chord moves in major and minor keys that provide a great starting point for songwriting. (Note to guitarists: a guitar-specific presentation of some of this material, with tab and video, is available in the *Acoustic Guitar* Guide titled *Songwriting Basics for Guitarists*.) Along the way, we'll check out common progressions used in many classic blues, rock, pop, folk, and country songs . . . and maybe your next song, too.

SONGWRITING BY NUMBER

The secret to understanding chord progressions is identifying chords in a progression by number—not by the letter names of the chords. This is the idea at work at a jam session when someone kicking off a song says, "It's I–IV–V in G," rather than, "The chords are G, C, and D." What these numbers do is describe the *function* of the chords no matter what key you're in; a I–IV–V in D works the same as a I–IV–V in G. When you're thinking of chords by number, you can quickly change a song's key, pinpoint what's happening in a cool chord sequence, or make connections between songs. You understand the musical logic, which in turn allows you to put that logic to work in your own songwriting.

This numbering system is based on the seven notes in the major scale, which are also called scale degrees, and numbered one through seven. This is the sequence of notes you will recognize as *do re mi fa sol la ti do* (watch *The Sound of Music* and sing along with "Do-Re-Mi" if you need a refresher). The first note of the scale is called the *root* (or simply the 1), and then we step up the scale by degrees until we arrive again at the root an *octave* higher (the same note at a higher frequency). Here's what the major scale looks like starting at the note C—otherwise known as a C major scale.

do	re	mi	fa	sol	la	ti	do
C	D	E	F	G	A	B	C
1	2	3	4	5	6	7	8 (or 1)

We create this *do re mi* sound by following a specific pattern of intervals, or distances between notes. Every major scale uses this same sequence of whole steps (on a guitar, the equivalent of two frets) and half steps (one fret).

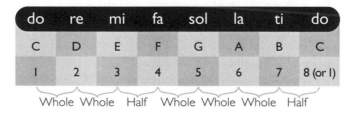

do	re	mi	fa	sol	la	ti	do
C	D	E	F	G	A	B	C
1	2	3	4	5	6	7	8 (or 1)

Whole Whole Half Whole Whole Whole Half

By starting on any note and following the same pattern of whole and half steps, we can create a major scale in any key.

Using any major scale, we can then build a chord off each scale degree by stacking two other notes in the scale on top: moving up the scale, we skip a note and use the next one, and then do the same again. To build a C-major chord from a C-major scale (C D E F G A B), we start with C, skip a scale degree to add E, then skip another scale degree to add G:

<u>C</u> D <u>E</u> F <u>G</u> A B
C–E–G = C major

To build a chord rooted on D, we start with the second scale degree and repeat the process, giving us a D-minor chord.

C <u>D</u> E <u>F</u> G <u>A</u> B
D–F–A = D minor

The same stacking pattern holds for all the scale degrees and for any major scale.

What we get by doing this are the diatonic chords—a family of chords that occur naturally in any major key. Even if you're not familiar with any of this theory, your ears recognize how diatonic chords fit together, because you've heard them at work in songs your whole life.

Take a look at the table "Diatonic Chords in Major Keys." The Roman numerals indicate the scale degree the chord is built on, as well as the type of chord: major chords are uppercase, and minor and diminished chords are lowercase (diminished chords are indicated with ° or *dim*). The I is the tonic or root chord and also the name of the key. No matter what key we're in, the I, IV, and V chords are major; the ii, iii, and vi are minor; and the vii° is diminished. This table includes all the keys, but the five most common ones (at least for guitar players) are highlighted.

In practice, this table shows that a straightforward song in the key of G, for instance, often uses only the chords in the G row: G, Am, Bm, C, D, Em, and (much less commonly) F#dim. In fact, many popular songs include only three or four of these diatonic chords. Out of the universe of chords, songwriters are often working with just a handful of options.

Diatonic Chords in Major Keys

I	ii	iii	IV	V or V7	vi	vii°
C	Dm	Em	F	G or G7	Am	Bdim
D♭	E♭m	Fm	G♭	A♭ or A♭7	B♭m	Cdim
D	Em	F♯m	G	A or A7	Bm	C♯dim
E♭	Fm	Gm	A♭	B♭ or B♭7	Cm	Ddim
E	F♯m	G♯m	A	B or B7	C♯m	D♯dim
F	Gm	Am	B♭	C or C7	Dm	Edim
G♭	A♭m	B♭m	B	D♭ or D♭7	E♭m	Fdim
G	Am	Bm	C	D or D7	Em	F♯dim
A♭	B♭m	Cm	D♭	E♭ or E♭7	Fm	Gdim
A	Bm	C♯m	D	E or E7	F♯m	G♯dim
B♭	Cm	Dm	E♭	F or F7	Gm	Adim
B	C♯m	D♯m	E	F♯ or F♯7	G♯m	A♯dim

BUILDING CHORDS IN MINOR KEYS. As with major keys, we find the diatonic chords in minor keys by using a scale—in this case, the main building block is the natural minor scale. The natural minor scale is the same as the major scale starting on the sixth note, or scale degree. If we take the C major scale (C D E F G A B) and start on the sixth (A), we get the A natural minor scale: A B C D E F G. We build a chord on each scale degree by stacking notes just as we did with the major scale, skipping a note and using the next one, and then doing the same again. So to build a chord off the first degree of the A-minor scale, we start with A, skip a scale degree to add C, then skip another scale degree to add E—those three notes form an Am chord. To build a chord rooted on B, we start with the second scale degree and repeat the process, giving us a Bdim chord: B–D–F.

A B C D E F G

A–C–E = A minor

A B C D E F G

B–D–F = B diminished

The same stacking pattern holds for all the scale degrees and for any minor scale.

THE NASHVILLE NUMBER SYSTEM

Roman numerals are traditionally used to represent chords by their function in a key, but many session players and other musicians prefer regular old Arabic numerals, using what's called the Nashville number system. Written this way, a I–IV–V progression is 1 4 5. Take a look at the sample chart for John Lennon's "Imagine." There are variations in how people chart songs using this system, but here's a primer on how it generally works.

Imagine   John Lennon
4/4, key of C

‖: 1 1△7 4 :‖   *play 4x*

4 6-   2- 2-7/1   5   57

‖: 4 5   1 37 :‖ *play 3x*

4 5   1

Each number is a major chord unless otherwise indicated. For other types of chords, add the conventional suffixes: *m* (or –) for minor; *dim* (or °) for diminished; *aug* (or +) for augmented; a small 7 for a seventh (as in 57); *maj7* (or △7) for a major seventh; and so on.

For chords with a note other than the root in the bass, use a slash with a number indicating the bass note. In "Imagine," the $2^{-7}/1$ is a 2 minor seventh chord (in the key of C, that's Dm7) with 1 (C) in the bass. Note that the number of the bass note refers to the key: in the $2^{-7}/1$, C is the 1 in the key of C.

With this system, each number stands for one measure. If a measure is split evenly between chords, underline the numbers (chords) that fall in the same measure. If a measure is split unevenly, indicate the beats with dots above the chords. That happens in the first measure of "Imagine": you hold C for three beats and C△7 for one beat.

A diamond shape (as appears above the 5^7 chord in "Imagine") means that you hold the chord and let it ring. For a chord that you accent and then mute, use a marcato symbol (^).

Finally, use pointy brackets above a chord to indicate syncopation: < means that the chord changes before the downbeat, and > means it changes after.

For repeats, ritards, and other directions, you can use the same symbols as in standard notation.

When we follow this pattern for all seven scale degrees, we wind up with the chords shown in "Diatonic Chords in Minor Keys." Again, the most common minor keys are highlighted.

Diatonic Chords in Minor Keys

i	ii° or ii	♭III	iv or IV	v or V	♭VI	♭VII
Am	Bdim or Bm	C	Dm or D	Em or E	F	G
A#m/ B♭m	B#dim or B#m/ Cdim or Cm	C#/ D♭	D#m or D#/ E♭m or E♭	E#m or E#/ Fm or F	F#/G♭	G#/ A♭
Bm	C#dim or C#m	D	Em or E	F#m or F#	G	A
Cm	Ddim or Dm	E♭	Fm or F	Gm or G	A♭	B♭
C#m	D#dim or D#m	E	F#m or F#	G#m or G#	A	B
Dm	Edim or Em	F	Gm or G	Am or A	B♭	C
D#m/ E♭m	E#dim or Em/ Fdim or Fm	F#/G♭	G#m or G#/ A♭m or A♭	A#m or A#/ B♭m or B♭	B/C♭	C#/ D♭
Em	F#dim or F#m	G	Am or A	Bm or B	C	D
Fm	Gdim or Gm	A♭	B♭m or B♭	Cm or C	D♭	E♭
F#m	G#dim or Gm	A	Bm or B	C#m or C#	D	E
Gm	Adim or Am	B♭	Cm or C	Dm or D	E♭	F
G#m/ A♭m	A#dim or A#m/ B♭dim or B♭m	B/C♭	C#m or C/ D♭m or D♭	D#m or D#/ E♭m or E♭	E/F♭	F#/G♭

When we build chords with the natural minor scale, the i, iv, and v are minor; the ii° is diminished; and the ♭III, ♭VI, and ♭VII are major. But as you see, the chart shows that the ii can also be minor, and the IV and V can be major. These alternatives occur because we can build chords with other minor scales, namely the harmonic and melodic minor, which have slightly different notes and create slightly different chords. The bottom line is you can pick which scales and chords to use, and the three alternatives shown are common choices for songwriting.

In the following sections we'll put these numbers to work and look at some common chord progressions and songs that use them.

PROGRESSIONS IN MAJOR KEYS

Let's use the number system to run through a few diatonic chord progressions in major keys, starting with the most basic.

JUST THE I. Some songs don't change chords at all—they simply hang out on the I (often, a bluesy I7 chord) and rely on the melody and groove to maintain musical interest. Here are a few famous examples. To hear these and other songs mentioned in these lessons on chord progressions, check out the playlists at completesingersongwriter.com.

> "Mannish Boy," Muddy Waters
> "Run Through the Jungle,"
> Creedence Clearwater Revival
> "Chain of Fools," Aretha Franklin
> (Don Covay)
> "Show Biz Kids," Steely Dan
> "Loser," Beck

Even though these songs don't change chords, the accompaniment still moves—often with a bass line or riff.

TRAIN YOUR EARS

If you're not accustomed to thinking of chord progressions by number, one of the best ways to learn is to say the numbers aloud while you're playing a song. Start with something simple—a three-chorder with a traditional sound—and each time you change chords, call out I, IV, V, or whatever the chords may be. Easy? Try a song with more chords or quicker changes. The more you practice this, the better you'll be at recognizing by ear the relationships between chords in a progression. Eventually, you'll reach a point where you can identify chords by number while listening to a recording, without referring to an instrument. Developing that ability is a real boon for a songwriter, because when you hear a song idea in your head, you'll be able to capture the progression whether or not there's a guitar or keyboard within reach.

I AND V. If a song adds just one more chord to the I, chances are it's the V. The move from V to I is fundamental—once the home-base I chord is established and a song goes to the V, our ears want it to resolve to the I. Rocking between I and V is more than enough tension and release on which to build a song, as proven by these classic examples.

> "Jambalaya," Hank Williams
> "Iko Iko," the Dixie Cups
> "Memphis, Tennessee," Chuck Berry
> "Men Smart (Women Smarter)," King Radio

I, IV, V. Add the IV chord to the I and V, and you've got the chord trinity behind countless songs. When people say all you need are three chords and the truth, these are the chords they mean. The I, IV, and V can appear in any order, as you can see in these examples.

"La Bamba," Richie Valens
I IV V

"Helpless," Neil Young
I V IV

"This Land Is Your Land," Woody Guthrie
IV I V I

TAKE VI. Venturing outside the I, IV, and V, the next diatonic chord you're likely to encounter is the vi. Many songs move between the I and vi—a smooth change because the chords have two of their three notes in common, as you can hear in "Shout."

"Shout," Isley Brothers
I vi / *bridge* I IV

One of the templates of early rock 'n' roll is I–vi–IV–V, used most famously in "Stand By Me."

"Stand By Me," Ben E. King (with Jerry Lieber and Mike Stoller)
I vi IV V

The same sequence is heard in the Beatles' "Octopus's Garden" and the Police's "Every Breath You Take" (in which the chords are dressed up with ninths for a jazzier sound). Reorder these four chords and you get the progressions for tons of other songs. Note that the following are examples, not complete chord charts—these songs have additional sections.

"Octopus's Garden," the Beatles
chorus I vi IV V

"Every Breath You Take," the Police
I vi IV V vi / I vi IV V I

"With or Without You," U2
"The Story," Brandi Carlile
I V vi IV

"Take Me Home, Country Roads," John Denver
chorus I V vi IV / I V IV I

"Let It Be," the Beatles
verse I V vi IV / I V IV I

By shuffling the I, IV, V, and vi around, changing how long you hold each chord, and trying different rhythmic feels, you can cover a tremendous amount of songwriting territory.

THE II AND III.   By adding the ii and iii chords to your songwriting palette, you can create seemingly infinite progressions. Here are some examples, including several drawn from the songbook of Bob Dylan. Notice how "I Shall Be Released" ascends the diatonic chords like a ladder: I–ii–iii to a quick IV–V. "Like a Rolling Stone" uses a similar pattern: the verses start with I–ii–iii–IV–V, hang for a couple lines on IV–V, and then go right back down, IV–iii–ii–I.

"Friend of the Devil," the Grateful Dead
verse I IV I IV
chorus V ii V ii V

"You Ain't Goin' Nowhere," Bob Dylan
I ii IV I

"I Shall Be Released," Bob Dylan
I ii iii IV V

"Like a Rolling Stone," Bob Dylan
verse I ii iii IV V *2x* / IV V IV V
IV iii ii I *2x* / ii IV V

In these examples you can see some common functions of the ii and iii:

ii leads to V or IV
iii leads to IV

With a good handle on the I, ii, iii, IV, V, and vi, you are ready to roll for writing in major keys—and you're also primed for our next topic, chord progressions in minor keys.

PROGRESSIONS IN MINOR KEYS

Minor keys are often said to be brooding and sad, but not all minor key songs are as bleak as, say, "Death Don't Have No Mercy." They can also be soothing (George Gershwin's "Summertime"), funky (the Commodores' "Brick House"), or upbeat and rocking (Dire Straits' "Sultans of Swing"). Chord progressions in minor keys provide a rich set of musical possibilities and should be part of every songwriter's palette.

So let's look at the diatonic chords in minor keys, and at common progressions and classic songs using those chords.

MINOR BLUES.   The major I, IV, and V are the kingpins in major keys, and their minor equivalents also figure prominently in minor keys. As noted in the section on diatonic chords in minor keys, the IV and V chords can be minor (written lowercase) or major (uppercase). You can see both variations in the following examples. Also notice that "The Thrill Is Gone" and "Unchain My Heart" use ♭VI–V instead of just V (more on the ♭VI chord below).

"Black Magic Woman," Santana (Peter Green)
i v i iv / i v i

"Evil Ways," Santana (Sonny Henry)
i IV *repeats until ending* V

"The Thrill Is Gone," B. B. King (Roy Hawkins/Rick Darnell)
i iv i / ♭VI V i

"Unchain My Heart," Ray Charles (Bobby Sharp)
i ♭VI i / iv i iv / ♭VI V i

THE ♭VII AND ♭III.   In minor-key songs, the ♭VII (with a root one whole step, or two frets on the guitar, below the i) and the ♭III (one and a half steps, or three frets, up from the i) often play a central role. These two classics use the same combo of the i and the ♭VII.

"Masters of War," Bob Dylan
"Working Class Hero," John Lennon
i ♭VII (*occasional* ♭VII IV i)

In a minor key, the ♭III is known as the relative major of i; these chords have two notes in common, so songs often move between them. In many songs the ♭III leads to the ♭VII.

"Jolene," Dolly Parton
i ♭III ♭VII i ♭VII i

"Another Brick in the Wall," Pink Floyd
verse i IV
chorus ♭III ♭VII i

THE ♭VI   Another important chord in minor keys is the ♭VI. To conjure its sound, think of "Eleanor Rigby."

"Eleanor Rigby," the Beatles
verse i ♭VI

Coming from the i, the ♭VI has an uplifting sound. Simon and Garfunkel's "The Sound of Silence," for instance, starts out with a somber i–♭VII–i (darkness is their old friend, after all) but then brightens when it goes to ♭VI–♭III.

"The Sound of Silence," Simon and Garfunkel
i ♭VII i
♭VI ♭III *3x*
i ♭III ♭VII i

DESCENDING FROM THE I.   In many minor songs where the ♭VI appears, the ♭VII is right with it. One classic sequence is i–♭VII–♭VI–♭VII, voiced so that the roots of the ♭VII and ♭VI are below the i.

"All Along the Watchtower," Bob Dylan
"Stairway to Heaven" (*climax*), Led Zeppelin
i ♭VII ♭VI ♭VII

Often, a descending i–♭VII–♭VI continues a half step lower, to the V. You can hear this sequence, for example, in the verses of "Stray Cat Strut" (in fact, the song modulates and follows the same descending pattern from the iv chord).

"Stray Cat Strut," Stray Cats
i ♭VII ♭VI V / *same pattern from* iv

The ♭VI–V (or ♭VI–v) move also pops up in songs that don't include the ♭VII.

"I Shot the Sheriff," the Wailers
chorus i iv
verse ♭VI v i

ALL TOGETHER NOW. Finally, let's fit these diatonic chords together in longer minor-key progressions.

"The House of the Rising Sun," the Animals (traditional)
i ♭III IV ♭VI / i ♭III V
i ♭III IV ♭VI / i V i

"Hotel California," the Eagles
verse i V ♭VII IV / ♭VI ♭III iv V
chorus ♭VI bIII V i / ♭VI ♭III iv V

Notice how "Hotel California" uses both the major IV and minor iv. In the chorus, we have the brightening move to the ♭VI followed by the same sequence that ends the verse (♭III–iv–V). The only diatonic chord not used is the ii.

WRITING IN MINOR KEYS. As the songs and progressions above suggest, you can use minor keys for a wide range of moods and effects in your songwriting. They do have an edge that may be just right for an emotionally dark song, but don't stereotype keys as "major = happy" and "minor = sad." If you marry heavy lyrics with heavy-sounding music, the result can be, well, heavy handed—the song bludgeons listeners rather than connecting with them. Instead, brighter major-key music might be worth trying for those same heavy lyrics—think of John Prine's "Sam Stone," with its tragic story of a drug-addicted veteran set over folky major-key fingerpicking. Conversely, setting lighter lyrics to darker music might give a song a more complex quality. Songs, like life experiences, are often filled with conflicting emotions.

MAKE YOUR OWN. These are just a few examples of what you can do with diatonic chords in major and minor keys. In the next few sections we'll look at chord substitutions and also nondiatonic chords—the chords from outside the key that can add harmonic surprise to a song. There's much more to explore, and really no limit to the variations you can create.

In any case, with an understanding of diatonic chords, you've got the basic vocabulary for a lifetime's worth of songs in your hands.

SIMPLE SUBSTITUTIONS

Let's say you're working on a song idea and playing some chords—you start on G, switch to C and back to G, go to D, and resolve to G. That chord progression sounds perfectly good but seems a little too familiar. You feel like you could be playing a thousand other songs, when your goal is to create something new. So how do you shake things up a bit to find a chord progression—and eventually a complete song—that feels and sounds like your own?

One great way is to use chord substitutions. Swapping out a chord or two can really liven up a progression and also help you discover new melodic ideas to sing on top. Particularly when you're working within the family of diatonic chords, which have many notes in common, you can make substitutions that subtly change the sound and mood of a progression while leaving intact its basic movement. Here are some simple substitutions you can try in your songwriting.

THE RELATIVES. The easiest kind of substitution is to swap a major chord with its relative minor, or a minor chord with its relative major. These pairs of chords are, as the names suggest, related: they have two of their three notes in common. For instance, a G major chord is made up of the notes G, B, and D; while its relative minor, Em, has the notes E, G, and B. So you can substitute an Em chord for a G major chord, or vice versa, for a smooth but noticeable change in the sound of the progression—and usually you can sing the same melody over either chord.

Take, for instance, the simple country/folk progression mentioned above:

I	IV	I	V
G	C	G	D

You could substitute an Em for the second G and play:

I	IV	vi	V
G	C	Em	D

Or you could split up the measures of G in the original version to create more movement in the progression:

I	vi	IV	vi	I	V
G	Em	C	Em	G	D

It's good to know we can swap G and Em chords, but for songwriting what we really want is to be able to make this type of substitution on any chord in any key. To accomplish that, the number system comes in handy. The relative minor of the I chord is the vi—and the same is true for the I and vi in any key.

There are other pairs of relative minors/majors within this diatonic chord family: ii is the relative minor of IV, and iii is the relative minor of V, so we can swap these chords as well. Again starting with the G–C–G–D progression, we can make these variations:

I	IV	I	V
G	C	G	D

I	ii	vi	V
G	Am	Em	D

I	vi	ii	vi	iii
G	Em	Am	Em	Bm

In the second variation, ending on the iii rather than the V leaves the progression feeling unsettled. That's a striking contrast to the happy-go-lucky I–IV–I–V and might suggest very different lyrical content.

Every major chord has a relative minor (and every minor chord has a relative major), and you can substitute one for the other no matter what key you're in. On the complete charts of diatonic chords you can find all these pairs—they are the I and vi in a major key, or the i and ♭III in a minor key. Here they are listed on their own.

Relative Minors

Major Chord	Relative Minor
C	Am
D♭	B♭m
D	Bm
E♭	Cm
E	C♯m
F	Dm
G♭	E♭m
G	Em
A♭	Fm
A	F♯m
B♭	Gm
B	G♯m

Memorize these relative major/minor pairs, and you'll have a whole bunch of possible substitutions in your songwriting toolbox.

Within the diatonic chord family, another good substitution to try is the iii for the I. In the key of G, that means substituting a Bm for a G, as shown in this variation on the progression we've been using.

I iii IV   I iii V
G Bm   C   G Bm   D

The iii makes a nice transition chord between the I and IV and between the I and V.

FLIPPING MINORS AND MAJORS. We can also substitute chords outside the diatonic family, sometimes called nondiatonic chords. These chords stand out more in a progression than diatonic chords do, because they include notes not in the scale of the song's key, and can be used to great effect. Here are a few examples that involve substituting major chords for the ii, iii, and vi— the diatonic minor chords in a major key.

First, compare these two progressions. The first has a minor ii (Am), and the second has a major II (A). Notice the contrast in sound even though only one note changes.

I   ii   V
G   Am   D
I   II   V
G   A   D

Coming from the I, the II (often played as a II7, a seventh chord) pulls strongly toward the V, and so is most often followed by a V. You can hear this II–V–I sequence in lots of country and bluegrass tunes—like this classic:

"Hey, Good Lookin'," Hank Williams
I II V7 I V7

Using the major III (or III7) instead of the diatonic minor iii has a similar effect as substituting the major II for the minor ii. Here are some notable examples.

"Freight Train," Elizabeth Cotten
I V7 I / III IV I V I

"On the Road Again," Willie Nelson
I III7 ii IV V

Using a major VI creates a strong ragtimey sound, as heard in these songs.

"Alice's Restaurant Massacre," Arlo Guthrie
I VI7 II7 V I

"Nobody Knows You When You're Down and Out," Eric Clapton
    (Jimmy Cox)
I III7 VI ii VI ii
IV I VI II7 V7

"(Sitting on) the Dock of the Bay," Otis Redding
chorus I VI I VI / I II I VI

In addition to turning diatonic minor chords into majors, you can do the opposite and turn diatonic majors into minors—such as replacing a diatonic major IV with a minor iv, or a diatonic major V with a minor v. The Beatles made brilliant use of these chords to differentiate sections of songs. The verse and chorus of "I Want to Hold Your Hand" have the V, but then the bridge ("And when I touch you . . .") kicks off with an arresting minor v. Similarly, "She Came in Through the Bathroom Window" uses I–IV in the verse and then I–iv in the bridge ("Didn't anybody tell her?").

"I Want to Hold Your Hand," the Beatles
chorus IV V I vi IV V I
bridge v I IV ii v I / IV V IV V IV V

"She Came in Through the Bathroom Window," the Beatles
verse I IV
bridge I iv *2x* / ♭VII ♭III ♭VII ♭III

Radiohead's "Creep" uses the major III as well as both the major IV and minor iv, to powerful effect.

"Creep," Radiohead
I III IV iv

As you experiment with substitutions in your songwriting, let your ears guide you. If you find a substitution that sounds good, pay attention to where the progression wants to go next. Good chord progressions have a momentum and direction of their own, and often the best songs come when you follow their lead.

BLUES/ROCK CHANGES

Go ahead: grab an open-position E chord on your guitar and give it a few good, hard strums. Do the same on a D chord and then an A. Get a steady rhythm going and keep circling around, E–D–A. Stand and sling your guitar down at your hips (or, better, knees); shades are optional but recommended.

The E, D, and A are what Patti Smith, in her memoir *Just Kids*, calls the classic rock chords—played by Lenny Kaye in Smith's seminal version of Van Morrison's "Gloria." Guitarists particularly love these chords since they can all be played in easy shapes with open bass strings. Many a garage band has been formed with not much more.

Part of what gives this chord progression its character is the D chord—which, viewed from the perspective of E major, is a ♭VII chord. Using the ♭VII gives a distinct blues/rock edge to a song in a major key, and there are two other related chords that have a similar effect: the ♭III and the ♭VI (in the key of E, these are G and C, respectively). Let's check out how these chords work, and how you can use them in your own songwriting.

Born in the blues.   The ♭III, ♭VI, and ♭VII chords are based in blues harmony, which plays with the tension between major and minor tonality. As discussed earlier in this chapter, each key has a set of naturally occurring diatonic chords. In the key of E major, for instance, the diatonic chords are as follows:

I	ii	iii	IV	V	vi	vii°
E	F♯m	G♯m	A	B	C♯m	D♯dim

And here are the diatonic chords in the parallel minor key, E minor:

i	ii°	♭III	vi	v	♭VI	♭VII
Em	F♯dim	G	Am	Bm	C	D

Notice that the ♭III, ♭VI, and ♭VII are diatonic chords in a minor key—not in a major key. So when we use these chords in a major-key song, we are borrowing chords from the parallel minor key. In essence, the ♭III, ♭VI, and ♭VII add a minor-key quality to a major-key song.

The chart "Blues/Rock Chords in Major Keys" shows the ♭III, ♭VI, and ♭VII chords, along with the diatonic I, ii, IV, and V chords.

Let's look at how these chords work in common progressions.

Blues/Rock Chords in Major Keys

I	ii	♭III	IV	V	♭VI	♭VII
C	Dm	E♭	F	G	A♭	B♭
C#/D♭	D#m/ E♭m	E/F♭	F#/G♭	G#/A♭	A/B♭♭	B/C♭
D	Em	F	G	A	B♭	C
E♭	Fm	G♭	A♭	B♭	C♭	D♭
E	F#m	G	A	B	C	D
F	Gm	A♭	B♭	C	D♭	E♭
F#/G♭	G#m/ A♭m	A/B♭♭	B	C#/D♭	D/E♭♭	E/F♭
G	Am	B♭	C	D	E♭	F
A♭	B♭m	C♭	D♭	E♭	F♭	G♭
A	Bm	C	D	E	F	G
B♭	Cm	D♭	E♭	F	G♭	A♭
B	C#m	D	E	F#	G	A

THE ♭VII. The ♭VII chord is widely used not just in blues and rock but folk, bluegrass, country, and more. Here are some examples using the I, ♭VII, and IV.

"Gloria," Them (Van Morrison)
I ♭VII IV

"That's What I Like About You," the Romantics
I IV ♭VII IV

"Franklin's Tower," the Grateful Dead
"Night Moves," Bob Seger (*verse*)
I ♭VII IV ♭VII

"Fire on the Mountain," the Grateful Dead
I ♭VII

If you're working on a song that uses the I, IV, and V, try substituting the ♭VII for the V to give the progression a different feel. In general, you can use the ♭VII to add zing to a progression otherwise made up of diatonic chords. For instance, the Allman Brothers' "Ramblin' Man" uses a I–♭VII–I in the beginning of the chorus ("Lord, I was born a ramblin' man") to make that line stand out in an otherwise standard country/folk progression with the diatonic I, IV, V, and vi chords.

"Ramblin' Man," the Allman Brothers
chorus I ♭VII I IV V / IV I vi IV I V I

Neil Young's "After the Gold Rush" has the same set of chords and accentuates the ♭VII to add to the song's mysterious mood.

"After the Gold Rush," Neil Young
I IV I IV / I V IV V
vi ♭VII IV ♭VII / I V ♭VII IV

THE ♭III. Add the bIII to a progression, and you can really start to rock out.

"After Midnight," J. J. Cale
I ♭III IV *2x*
I ♭III IV V / I ♭III IV I

"50 Ways to Leave Your Lover," Paul Simon
chorus I ♭III IV I

"Back in the USSR," the Beatles
verse I IV ♭III IV
chorus I ♭III IV

The ♭III also works well with the ♭VII in a progression. One example in a country vein is "Amie," which uses the ♭III en route to the IV and V.

"Amie," Pure Prairie League
verse I ♭VII IV *4x*
IV ♭lll IV ♭III V

THE ♭VI. The ♭VI chord is most often heard in edgy rock tunes. One function of the ♭VI is to lead to the V, before resolving to the I. You can hear this in J. J. Cale's "Cocaine," which in the refrain ("She don't lie . . .") uses the descending line I–♭VII–♭VI–V. On guitar, this sequence is easy to visualize with barre chords: from the I chord (say, an E barre chord at the seventh fret), slide down two frets to the ♭VII, down two more frets to the ♭VI, and, finally, down one more fret to the V.

"Cocaine," J. J. Cale
verse I ♭VII
refrain I ♭VII ♭VI V

You'll also find the ♭VI in a common chord sequence moving up the neck: from a ♭VI barre chord, go up two frets to the ♭VII, and up two more frets to the I. John Fogerty uses this ♭VI–♭VII–I sequence in "The Old Man Down the Road" on the title phrase.

"The Old Man Down the Road," John Fogerty
chorus I7 ♭VI ♭VII I7

ALL TOGETHER. One classic song that gives these blues/rock chords a complete workout is the Kinks' "All Day and All of the Night." The signature riff uses speedy barre-chord slides to and from the ♭VII (two frets below the I) and the ♭III (three frets above the I).

"All Day and All of the Night," Kinks
♭VII I ♭VII ♭III I

From there, the song transitions via the ♭VI and ♭VII to the same sliding-barre-chord riff starting from the II chord (down two frets to I, up three frets to IV) and then the V chord (down two frets to IV, up three frets to ♭VII). It's a very inventive—and totally rocking—way to use these chords.

As you work on your own songs, try substituting the ♭III, ♭VI, or ♭VII into a diatonic progression that sounds a little ho-hum—they may be just what you need to shake things up. You can use these chords for just a touch of bluesiness, as in "Ramblin' Man," or for full-tilt rock 'n' roll, as in "All Day and All of the Night." These chords will change not only the accompaniment but also your melodic options—your voice can play in the zone between major and minor just as your instrument does.

ON THE DRAWING BOARD

Sure, it happens: lightning strikes, and within a miraculously short time you've got a new song. You sputter trying to explain . . . It's like the song writes itself, just appears out of the ether and floats right through your instrument and voice—you almost feel sheepish taking credit for it. And the song is so sure of what it's saying and why it's here—every note and syllable just seems *right*. All you can do is sit back and gaze with admiration at this amazing gift.

Sure, it happens—and hallelujah when it does. But most of the time whole songs don't appear by divine intervention. They arrive piece by piece, over days or weeks or months, or as nominally complete songs that actually consist of a few really good parts and then some filler that basically sets up the good stuff and finally a couple of things that make you cringe. In other words, yup, you've got editing and rewriting ahead. In fact, many songwriters feel that reworking the material that needs it puts you in a position to receive the coveted songs that arrive in finished form.

> *I think unless you're willing to do your homework on the hard ones, the easy ones don't come.*
>
> —GREG BROWN

In this chapter we'll look at some strategies for turning those promising but problematic works-in-progress into finished songs—on your own and with help from others.

THE EDITING PROCESS

Editing and rewriting require a different mind-set than the one you used to chase down your original inspiration. Think of the creator and the editor as separate personas. You, the creator, have an idealized version in your head of what this song is or should be; you, the editor, respond to the actual notes and words from the perspective of a listener hearing the song for the first time, and you ask the tough questions about whether the song really delivers the goods. Ever practical and even hardheaded, the editor scrutinizes every detail of the song and wonders, is this really necessary? Could this part be stronger, more vivid, more concise? While the creator has all sorts of personal attachments to what has been written, the editor has to be prepared to cut perfectly good stuff, perhaps even great stuff, because it simply doesn't serve the song.

> With all of my songs, I write as much as I can in forty-eight hours. And then after forty-eight hours, if you have a rough draft of the song, you go back and you sharpen your pencil and get your eraser, because the editing is where a song goes from being a B or C song to being an A song. You ask yourself, what's the mission statement of the song? Even if it's a personal song, even if you're writing about isolation or loneliness or longing or love, what is the song trying to say? You put that on the top of the paper, and then you have to weigh how you can support the mission statement by improving every line.
>
> —ELLIS PAUL

To be an effective editor, you need some distance from your creation. When inspiration first strikes, you should spill out and record as much stuff as you can *without* filtering too much; that'll give you lots of material to work with later. Then take a break, and come back fresh and ready to be an editor. Record your work-in-progress if you haven't already, and as you listen back, try to imagine that you're hearing and critiquing someone else's work. Which parts really turn you on, and where do you start twiddling your thumbs or thinking about how you need to go grocery shopping?

This isn't always easy to do with your own song, which is why so many songwriters look to co-writers and friends to be sounding boards for their ideas (see "Collaborating" for insights into how the team approach works). But you can learn to be an effective editor, and your songs will surely benefit. The editing process varies from song to song, but here are some ideas about where to look for weak links and how to strengthen them.

HIT THE GROUND RUNNING. The song form is extremely concise, and you need to grab your audience's ear right from the first note and syllable. Some opening lines are real showstoppers (for instance, John Gorka's "I'm from New Jersey, I don't expect too much / If the world ended today, I would adjust"), but you don't necessarily have to dazzle people with your cleverness. The critical thing is just to start painting the scene, revealing something about the character or the emotion, setting the story in motion. If the opening lines amount basically to throat clearing, and the song's real statement doesn't arrive until verse two or three or the chorus, consider whether that later section might actually work in the beginning. In the writing process, sometimes you need to write preliminary stuff that helps you figure out what you're really trying to say—and then once you've figured that out, you should leave the preliminary stuff behind.

On the musical side, does your song start off strong and distinctive or does it sound like a thousand other songs? There are certain intros (mid-tempo strumming on the I chord, a standard 4/4 rock drum pattern by itself for a couple measures before the band kicks in) that have been done so many times that they make listeners' minds wander immediately, and you may never get their attention back. Try playing your song without its introduction—just skip right to the first verse—and see if you are really missing anything important. You might be able to take a more interesting chord move or riff from later in the song and use that as the intro, or in some cases you can just lop off much or all of your introduction and get things rolling more quickly.

MAKE MORE FROM LESS. Imagine that you're packing for a trip and you're allowed to bring only one small suitcase. You've got piles of stuff all over the bed that you think might be nice to have along (What if it happens to snow in June? What if I get invited to a black-tie party?), but there's no way it'll all fit. What do you truly need to bring? Separating the extraneous from the essential can be hard, but think how great you'll feel traveling so lightly.

So it is in songwriting: your song doesn't have to be short and simple, but every part of it is important and has to contribute to your main idea. And the less clutter you have overall, the more attention people will pay to what remains. This means you have to ask yourself questions such as, have I taken three verses to say what I could say in one?

> *I think it's a great challenge to try to be concise with writing a song. Any songwriter with a certain degree of experience can get an idea across—it may take five verses or whatever. We challenge ourselves to be really concise and really clear in what we're saying. . . . We'll combine verses—we'll take the first two lines of one verse and the last two lines of another. . . . We are not afraid to merge songs together to make one better song: take three different song ideas—what you think are three different songs—and make them one. It's exciting on the quality level and very sad on the quantity level.*
>
> —ED ROBERTSON

The same principles apply to the way you use language within an individual line. When you want to make an image more vivid, it is always tempting to pile on descriptive words, but they start to compete with each other so that the listener doesn't get a clear picture at all. Watch out for mixed metaphors: the love that's "solid as a rock" in one moment and makes you "soar" the next. Trim back to the one word or image that counts: instead of "the blazing, burning fire," just say "the flame." Extend or complement the images you have already used rather than introduce completely new ones. When I am editing words in this way, I picture a tree after a winter storm with its branches bent down nearly to the ground from the snow: I'm taking a shovel and knocking the snow off in clumps, and the limb rises as the weight falls off, eventually springing back to its natural shape.

You have to be economical on the musical side, too. Sometimes songs have an extra section that they are better off without, or maybe an instrumental part that sounds cool but is a distraction from the story you're trying to tell. On a micro level, there might be some lag time that you can cut.

Take inspiration from the original country blues players, who were not beholden to any 12-bar blues formula. They freely added and dropped beats or measures, changed chords when it felt right, cut a line short here, extended a line there. Go where your song wants to go, when it wants to go there.

I feel more and more like editing is the most important part of writing songs—cutting out the stuff that doesn't need to be there. I float songs by band members, and I have a little songwriting group with three other songwriters who write in different styles. We present these songs early on and get a response: Is there enough of the story? Is there something that can be taken out? We're kind of brutal with each other. To me, the longer you write songs, the easier it is to cut things out. I hear other people's songs and I'm always thinking, yeah, they're going on too long.

—KATHY KALLICK

SHOW IT. In lyrics, a specific action or thing or piece of dialogue has so much more power than a summary or explanation. You can say that a character is upset, but if he punches through a windowpane, we really see it. You can say she left him, but if he's breathing a cloud of exhaust in an empty driveway, we really taste it.

A friend of mine who is a great songwriter studied poetry in college, and one of her teachers said when you write, you should be able to pick up the page and shake it and have all this stuff fall off of it. Things, you know, shoes, cars, wheelbarrows, windows, cigarettes, ashtrays, whatever— things should be in there. When you put those kinds of things in, it makes a better picture; there's more stuff to grab onto. The message itself might be abstract—you may not even understand in the end what the heck the song is about, but there is a lot of stuff you have taken away and put in your pocket. Whereas with other songs, you can follow it completely, one word after the other, but by the time you get done, it's just a piece of stale bread.

—KELLY JOE PHELPS

Notice how he called it "a piece of stale bread" rather than an understandable but forgettable song?

Jeff Tweedy is another artist who feels that capturing these kinds of sharp details is the most important job of a lyricist. I once asked him whether he even aimed to have his lyrics make sense to a listener.

> *That's not really a goal, to be honest. I don't find a lot of my favorite lyricists to be perfect sense makers. Writing something that has an image, something that you see and you're not just being told about, is the main goal. And I can't dictate what you feel, but I want to feel something for myself. As long as that's happening, I really don't feel compelled to sweat just having it sound rational. Music isn't really supposed to play on that part of your brain; it's supposed to be more mythos or some sort of release from making sense.*
>
> —JEFF TWEEDY

In editing, look for places where you're telling the listener how someone feels or summarizing a story development, and replace those pieces with specific and evocative details. What's the character wearing or drinking or saying? What season is it? What memory is flashing through his or her mind? What smell is in the air?

> *You're trying to show. You can think of a character as being frustrated and depressed; these are conceptual things. But in order to write the character in a song, you can't tell the audience he's depressed—you have to show it. That's something all of my favorite songs have and something I aspire to in all of my songs is creating a little bit of a snow globe, so people are looking into it and then suddenly they're inside it—they're part of the song. They've escaped from their life into the song's life.*
>
> —ELLIS PAUL

BE FEARLESS. Sometimes in a draft of a song you are circling around a thorny, awkward, potentially embarrassing, or otherwise touchy subject, never really addressing it directly. The story wants to go there—and so does the listener—but you've hesitated (OK, chickened out a little). In the editing process, ask yourself whether you can go further or deeper, and take a little more risk. That is ultimately the job of an artist.

JEFF TWEEDY

I mean otherwise, why bother writing? Any form of expression, that's why you do it. It's a place where you don't have to be squeamish in any way. There's nobody looking over your shoulder; there's nobody telling you that you can't say that or that's inappropriate. If you listen to what's inside and let that come out, that seems like the thing to trust.

—DAN BERN

You've got to get close to the bone, otherwise what's the point of listening? I mean there's reggae and all sorts of music that you just want to dance to, but the kind of music that I do, why would anybody want to listen to me if I wasn't getting a little closer to the bone than they can get themselves?

—FERRON

TELL A STORY.   You may not be telling a dramatic or bawdy tale, but the song is a storytelling vehicle, and even mood songs should evolve from beginning to end.

> *In a short story you've got essentially what happens in a novel in an incredibly condensed form. There is some sense of change—some kind of an epiphany, or an ending that is uplifting or downturning. You don't know where you're going, but you know that you are on a journey that you trust when you're reading. It's the same thing in a song: you trust in the song to take you somewhere that you may or may not expect.*
> —STEVEN PAGE

Chances are you do have in mind some kind of movement or change or revelation that happens between your first verse and the final chorus. But the bottom line is, does your listener really get it? You might be projecting things into your song that are not really there or that are just too subtle for anyone but you to notice. Try making your plot line more explicit, and consider whether there are parts of the song that simply don't move the story along. Perhaps cutting some material in the middle would open up the room for you to write an extra verse or two and bring your story to a real climax.

CONSIDER THE POINT OF VIEW.   Make sure you haven't inadvertently changed point of view or person in your song—switching from *I* to *you* or *she* without even being conscious of it. Also, think about who is narrating your song and follow that person's perspective, because the same events look different through different eyes. The narrator's language and choice of detail should reveal something of his or her own character even if the story is about someone else. If there is nothing revealing about the narrator's perspective, why is that person telling the story?

Sometimes you can end a songwriting stalemate by changing the point of view or the narrator. For instance, if you are writing in first person, you may feel too obliged to be true to the facts of your own experience. Switching the entire song over to *he* or *she* (even temporarily) may free up your imagination to conjure the best story possible, while remaining "true" to the emotions that sparked it in the first place.

When something rings true, it doesn't even have to be biographically correct. I wrote a song that was a No. 1 hit for Willie Nelson called "There's Nothing I Can Do About It Now." At the time, Willie's whole marriage had blown up and he was getting a divorce, and he was just shifting so many things in his life. He wasn't writing, but he was making this record. . . . The lines of the song are written from a male standpoint: "I see the fire of a woman's scorn turn her heart of gold to steel," all these descriptive kind of Willie Nelson–esque lines. But the feeling of the song, the emotional place of the person singing the song, was really ringing true from my own experience.

You are not limited to an exact replica of what you wrote in your diary. You can go beyond the parameters of your own experience and yet use the emotions that you have experienced. That's what I have become most interested in as a songwriter. It's like I am not doing it alone. It's as if I opened this channel and all this assistance comes through—that sounds very new age, but it is magical. And I end up learning something from my own songs a lot of the time.

—Beth Nielsen Chapman

Go beyond your diary. As Chapman suggested, you might be able to improve a song by making it less narrowly autobiographical. Chris Thile once told me about an emotionally wrenching song called "You Don't Know What's Going On" that he'd started writing while going through divorce. He couldn't get the song right and eventually shelved it. Years later, when he revisited the idea with his Nickel Creek bandmates Sara and Sean Watkins, he was able to approach it more as an observer—and quickly finished it.

I felt like the song got new life with the fact that it was no longer really a song about me. To be honest, I hardly even remembered what that guy was so angry about, so I could go in and fix up the story.

To me, there's very little interest in a song that personal. I think that people should be able to tell their own stories through the songs that you write. Even if personal experience is the first mover, [the song] can't purely exist as this couch time for you with your audience as your therapist—I think that's insufferable. The great lyricists of our time find a way to help us tell our own stories with their lyrics.

—CHRIS THILE

LOOK AT THE BRIGHT SIDE.   Not every song needs to be "Zip-a-Dee-Doo-Dah," but if your song is unrelentingly bleak, consider whether you might shine a little light in it, for the sake of your listeners and for yourself.

I've always tried to put myself in place of an audience member, mainly because I was an audience member for so long. I can totally relate to the songwriters who've had pain and are going through hard times, and I can totally relate to how that comes out in their music because that's what they're feeling. But as an audience member, I personally didn't want to hear about people's problems. Just like everyone, I had my own problems, but when I went out I wanted to be entertained, I wanted to be taken away from the problems. So I always try to stay on the lighter side of things.

—KELLER WILLIAMS

The same holds true when you're writing a song to convey a political or social message, or to stir people to act against injustice: Don't take yourself too seriously, as a songwriter famous for his politically edged lyrics once explained.

I think a sense of humor, particularly if it's aimed at yourself, is crucial in any kind of songwriting. If you can make an audience laugh, put them at ease a bit, then you can—if you want to—deliver quite a strong political message. It's also a way of making the audience realize that you don't think you've got all the answers. You're just a singer-songwriter, and all you're really doing is focusing their solidarity, supplying their soundtrack. If the audience wants to change the world, you must let them know that it's their responsibility, not yours. Otherwise, you're betraying the trust of the audience, and you're kidding yourself as well.

—BILLY BRAGG

Humor does more than humanize you as an artist—it creates surprise and contrast. If your song just settles into a mood and stays there for the duration, with no twists to the story or in the music, perhaps you need to find a way to shake things up a bit. For Loudon Wainwright III, writer of some of the saddest *and* funniest songs around, surprising the audience is a crucial part of his job as a writer and performer.

> *Everybody develops a style as they go along. They write what they write about. Along the way I appreciated both aspects of the serious and the*

LOUDON WAINRIGHT III

not-so-serious, and I found a way to do both—in some cases in one song. It's a way to unsettle the audience a little bit, which brings them in closer, makes them pay more attention. They're not so relaxed and thinking, oh, this is a sad, mopey little song. If there's a laugh in the middle of it, they wake right up.

—Loudon Wainwright III

Allow yourself to be simple. As counterintuitive as it seems, one of the greatest challenges in songwriting is to be simple—which is not the same thing as being simple minded or simplistic. When a simple, direct expression pops up, you might greet it with skepticism, thinking that this idea must be trite or overused. Shouldn't a song be craftier than that? Well, not always. Several artists have told me that songs they initially thought were too obvious turned out to be favorites of their audiences. Those songs are easy to remember and easy to sing and communicate effortlessly, a quality that Pete Seeger admired in the work of his old traveling partner Woody Guthrie.

I tell you, I learned the genius of simplicity. He didn't try to get fancy, he didn't try to show how clever he was, and he was leery of trying a lot of chords. Even songs that literately demanded a double dominant—that is, a super tonic—he would not do it. Like "Do Re Mi," he used the tune of a country song, "Hang out the front door key, babe / Hang out the front door key," and if you're playing in G, you should hit an A major 7 there. Woody refused to. He was rebelling against all that cleverness, and he would hit a plain D7.

—Pete Seeger

The most interesting sorts of commercial music are the ones that find an emotion and put it out there. It might not be that subtly done; it might be kind of crude. But when a commercial writer finds an emotion and is able to articulate it in such a way that it's really clear, then everybody gets it and everybody wants to hear it. There's a skill, but it's in the background— it's not the first thing you hear. The first thing you hear is the emotion. . . . I think in the singer-songwriter genre, sometimes the intellect takes over a little too much and everybody gets a little too clever.

—Stephen Fearing

In a song, just as the music can get bogged down by ambitions and self-conscious cleverness, the lyrics can try too hard to be poetic. In reality, songs and poems are very different things. Dense language and complicated constructions might work on the page but sound clunky in a song, blocking the flow of the music.

> *Songwriting has a very defined structure, and it almost always sounds better when it rhymes or has some sort of internal rhyming. I find that if I take poetry and put it to music, it doesn't work, because it doesn't fit the structure that a song needs—it needs to have four lines pretty much, and a chorus that recurs. Poems don't revolve around that at all.*
>
> —Jewel

MAKE THE MELODY STAND ON ITS OWN.   One very common weakness is for the melody to be too closely tied to the chord progression (especially if the chords were written first). Play your song chord by chord and see how the

JEWEL

melody relates to the chords beneath it. Is the melody note frequently the root note of the chord? Does the melody tend to move when the chords move and stay put when the chords stay put? When you sing the song a cappella, does the melody sound weak? Doubling the melody with the accompaniment part (as in old blues and mountain ballads) can have a powerful effect, but the melody has to run the show.

It's surprisingly easy to lift a melody free from the chord progression, just by moving some parts of it off the dominant chord tones (especially the root) and varying the phrasing. Particularly sweet melodic passages often are the result of the songwriter stretching beyond the notes that are specifically in the accompanying chords. Lately I've been playing "Singin' in the Rain" in the key of F, and the accompaniment basically swings between F and C7 (I and V). While picking out the melody on my guitar, I noticed that the melody keeps falling to a D, which is not part of either chord but harmonizes nicely with both (making the F sound like an F6 and the C7 sound like a C9). Much of the character of that melody comes from that one inspired note choice.

BUILD CONTRAST BETWEEN SECTIONS. If you are using a verse-chorus form, the chorus is your moment to stand and deliver a ringing declaration, the words and music you most want your audience to go home singing. So the two sections shouldn't blur together too much: the chorus melody should rise higher than the verse, for instance, or use different phrase lengths or rhythms, or a different rhyme scheme. You might be able to rewrite the chorus melody to make it stand out more, or you might tinker with the chord progression by substituting an individual chord or moving into a different key center.

If the verse-chorus/verse-chorus/verse-chorus form is getting monotonous, you might need to add in a section, perhaps a full-on bridge or an instrumental solo. Even a short break can refresh your listeners' ears and let the most important parts of your song sink in.

WATCH THE TRANSITIONS. On the other hand, maybe you are trying to join two sections that are *too* different from each other. One tip-off that there's a problem is an awkward or abrupt transition; it sounds like you're driving too fast around a sharp curve. If you have incorporated an old idea that you have always wanted to use in a song, be sure that it really belongs, that you're not just being opportunistic. Great songs have a natural flow; one idea grows out of another and into the next.

When you are adding a new section to a song, try revamping or extending the elements from what you have already written (melody, chords, images) rather than interjecting something completely new. When you build from within like that, your whole song will have a satisfying coherence.

Sɪɴɢ ɪᴛ ʟɪᴋᴇ ʏᴏᴜ'ᴅ sᴘᴇᴀᴋ ɪᴛ.   Joni Mitchell once sang to me three different versions of the line "Since I lost you" (from her song "Man from Mars," which she was in the middle of recording at the time) to show how you can adjust the melody to make the emphasis fall on the most important word (in this case, *lost*), the way we do when we speak. This relationship between the words and the music is sometimes called prosody. When the prosody is right on (Mitchell cited Paul McCartney's musical setting of the word *yesterday* as an example), we don't even think about it, because the language just sounds so natural.

One of my self-imposed rules about lyrics is that there is very little that I would put into a song that I would not put into a conversation. It might be a fairly stylized conversation, but it wouldn't seem entirely out of place in a colloquy between two people or somebody expounding on the subject. I don't use archaic forms, I don't reverse word order to get a rhyme, and I try never to mispronounce words in order to get a metrical fit—you know, the emphasis on the wrong syl-la-ble, as it were.

On a lot of the songs that I do, I feel like I'm trying to get some fairly complicated ideas across in three minutes or four minutes, and in order to do that, the lyrics just have to flow. They have to sound natural, and I work on that.

—Cʜʀɪs Sᴍɪᴛʜᴇʀ

When I was getting ready to record my first piece of radio journalism, my editor at NPR made the excellent suggestion that I print out my script, highlight the most important words in each sentence, and then make sure

I emphasized those words when I read them aloud. That's a good exercise for lyrics too: write them out, highlight the critical words purely from a reader's perspective, and see if those are the same words that are emphasized in the music. Small adjustments to how you sing a line or structure a verse make a big difference.

MAKE SURE YOU'RE BARKING UP THE RIGHT TREE. If you have identified a problem line in your song but just can't make any headway in fixing it, you may be focusing on the wrong place: for example, the fact that you can't find a good rhyme in one line might mean that you need to change the previous line that you are trying to rhyme with. In other words, everything that leads up to a particular line in the song defines your options for what to write there, and if you change the lead-in, your problem may just disappear. It's like tuning a guitar: if the second string seems to be out of tune, there is a good chance that the third string is actually out of tune and making its neighbor sound bad. Once you address the real trouble spot, the second string sounds fine.

WORK ON IT IN THE BACKGROUND. I find that an effective way to fix small song-writing problems is to idly think about them while I'm doing something else—driving, walking, cooking. Several artists have told me they work out solutions while they sleep, which is a neat trick. When you are less focused on the task of songwriting and feeling less pressure, your mind may stumble upon a solution that eluded you when you were sweating it out in front of your notebook and your instrument, or at least you might come up with some new approaches that you can try in your next concentrated songwriting session.

> One place I really like to think about songs is the car. So I'll keep a pencil and paper in the car, and if I'm working on something and I have a demo, I'll put that in the car and just listen to it. It's something about left brain/ right brain—I'm having to look at the road and make the turns, and listening at the same time kind of frees me up. I can't explain it. Problems get solved that way.
>
> —SHAWN COLVIN

FINALLY, BEWARE OF RULES. Everywhere you turn, someone will be happy to tell you (or, actually, sell you) the rules of songwriting, the secret behind every No. 1 hit of the last fifty years. But the way in which your song breaks a rule or defies a formula could be its best quality. The goal of editing is not to make your song conform, but to understand what it is trying to say and to do whatever you can to make that statement ring loud and clear. You are spotlighting the strengths and cutting back the weaknesses. Above all, you are listening to where the song wants to go.

The editing process can involve some very rational and pragmatic thinking, but you also need to respect the mysteries and ambiguities inherent in all art. Songs, like our lives, ripple outward into things that we may feel or sense but not understand. It sounds paradoxical, but you are trying to be very specific in evoking what may be ultimately inexplicable.

> *It's a good thing to not pretend that you understand everything. You can write a song or sing a song about something and actually leave it saying, "I don't know what this is about." You're singing about your confusion about it, the fact that it's a mystery to you. That's a good thing because that's a true thing. You don't understand everything. When you sing about relationships, I don't know how you can tie it up in the end because so much of it is not understandable.*
>
> —KELLY JOE PHELPS

COLLABORATING

Opening up your songwriting process to another person might seem like a scary prospect (my baby!), but it can do wonders for your songs. A collaborator might see a problem that needs attention or a solution that has eluded you, suggest approaches that never occurred to you, or simply encourage you to keep chasing down a great idea. There are many levels of collaboration, from asking a friend, "Hey, what do you think of this?" to full-on co-writing. Here are some thoughts on what a collaborator can bring to the process, along with testimonials from singer-songwriters who have written both solo and with others.

SOUNDING BOARD.   There's a time in writing by yourself when you lose all perspective on what you're doing—you have two options and you are not sure which one is better; there's a section in the song that drives you nuts, but you just can't figure out how to fix it; you no longer have any idea whether the song is saying what you want it to say or if it's any good at all. The solution? Ask someone you trust—a friend with a good ear, a spouse, another musician, a fellow songwriter, anyone who is sympathetic but also not afraid to tell it like it is.

> *I run a song by them and they will make a suggestion—that line doesn't work, or why don't you get rid of that word, or use this word instead of that word, or put that verse up top, that kind of thing. Or sometimes it's just encouragement to keep writing it—"That's worth working on."*
>
> *I think most songwriters come up at least against questions: What about this line? Is this line better? Or you might really get stuck and need somebody to just show you the door and make you realize that there are a lot more options.*
>
> —LOUISE TAYLOR

Oddly, sometimes the simple act of playing a new song for someone can help with the editing process, even if the other person doesn't have any specific or useful suggestions. Sharing your song like this allows you to hear it in a different way. Sara Watkins has been playing music with her brother, Sean, since they were little kids in Nickel Creek, and she described how he helps her finish songs without saying a word.

> *He's generally one of the first people I play a song for if I have a new idea. Very often I don't even need feedback. The other day I had a song and I was like, "I have this thing; I don't really want any feedback yet, I just need to play it for you." I played it for him and I was like, "Thanks—now I know what I need to do in this song." When you play it for somebody you respect, it just makes the stakes a little higher, and you notice, oh, that lyric that I was trying to overlook really stands out like a sore thumb.*
>
> —SARA WATKINS

Singer-songwriters who cultivate these kinds of relationships often find that they become indispensable: they streamline the writing process and encourage tighter, more mature songs.

I don't know how people write without an editor. It's so much easier when someone says to you, "Look, that line is not good" or "That's a cliché" or "You can make that better" or "That line really is good." It's incredibly helpful.

—Lucy Kaplansky

A bandmate or performing partner is an obvious candidate to be a sounding board. That person already understands and helps shape your music onstage, and sharing your embryonic songs gets him or her in on the ground floor. Here's how the Indigo Girls duo described the kind of feedback they give each other during the editing and arranging process.

We'll ask, "What do you think of this?" and the other person might say, "I think the chorus is too long" or "I think we should add a bridge" or "I'm missing this element." If the song's important enough for the person to have written it and believe in it themselves, then you've got to give it a chance.

—Amy Ray

You have to have faith that the process is working. You have to get used to someone else's ideas being added to your song. You're used to just singing it alone and you know the song in an intimate and personal way, and then all of a sudden it's become something else. But I have faith in what Amy and I have done for so long, and while sometimes it's an adjustment at first, in the end the song usually comes out being better.

—Emily Saliers

Sharing a new song like this will not only bring out good ideas for improvements, but it gives your bandmate a stronger connection to the material. That feeling of buy-in is crucial for any band, as Joey Ryan of the Milk Carton Kids explained.

We're both just trying to write songs that we both feel comfortable singing and playing for the next two years, because we both have to stand onstage playing these songs and singing them as though they're our own. A lot of times, one or the other of us writes the song but the other one ends up

AMY RAY AND EMILY SALIERS, INDIGO GIRLS

singing the melody and becomes the narrator and the person who has to
believe it and feel as though it represents them.

—JOEY RYAN

CO-WRITING.   Co-writing is the most complete form of collaboration: two
songwriters meeting on equal ground and bringing their individual talents
to bear on a collective creation. You co-write to stretch beyond your own

capabilities, complement your strengths with someone else's strengths, and explore styles you couldn't really pull off on your own. This relationship could last for only one song or for an entire career. When a great songwriter discovers his or her musical soulmate, the results can be magical (Rodgers and Hammerstein, Lieber and Stoller, Goffin and King, Lennon and McCartney, Garcia and Hunter, and so on).

Singer-songwriters who have worked solo for years are often surprised by what happens when they try co-writing.

It's a little terrifying. I'm fairly insecure, and I think most songwriters are, that maybe the person is going to laugh at your ideas or find them dumb. But with every co-writing experience that I've had, bar none, we came up with a song, and I've pretty much recorded all of them. Now I don't know if that means my filter is too big or that I've just been very lucky.

I had a built-in default snobbery about co-writing, which was, that's what you do when you're running out of steam and just before you make a kid's record. It was really that kind of mentality. I've found it to be so completely the opposite. The true nature of collaboration is the other person's energy and your energy coming together, and at some point in the creative writing process you get so caught up in the excitement of creating something with a sort of a stranger that all the boundaries drop and everybody starts giggling and making cups of tea and papers are all over the desk. I love that. I go home from those sessions and feel like I am twenty feet tall, and I end up writing more material on my own. So it's been nothing but a good thing for me.

—Stephen Fearing

I think we get really precious as writers and artists that somehow our technique is a secret, or if we tell someone we're not going to be able to do it again. So to turn it around [with co-writing] is really revelatory. If you just do it a lot and with different people and in different incarnations, you find out that there are rules you can follow and it's not really magic. And when it is magic, to have somebody else witness it is pretty cool.

—Natalia Zukerman

In a good co-writing relationship, you and your partner sense the potential in each other's ideas and help develop and expand them in ways you individually could not have done. This is how Steve Martin described co-writing with Edie Brickell, where she wrote vocal melodies and lyrics for his banjo instrumentals.

> *The truth is, in these songs, I knew there was a story; I didn't know what it was at all, and Edie found it. I've always felt the banjo carried emotion, from the first time I heard it. It's taken me fifty years of playing to be able to play in a way to state those emotions. So I feel like the tunes I wrote were circling around the emotions of America and these stories, and Edie was able to translate them into words.*
>
> —STEVE MARTIN

Bob Weir of the Grateful Dead explained how, depending on the nature of the original inspiration, he looks for different sorts of contributions from a co-writer.

> *As a lyricist, I can generally get the job done, but I'm glacially slow, so I like to work with people who have a little more facility with that. Or I may have a general notion of the color of the rhythm and the harmonic or melodic development, and I'll sit with a guy and we just fire blank verse at each other until we start to corner that color—and then often the song will fall right out of the sky. Other times, I may have no notion of where the song wants to go, in which case I'll let whoever I'm working with surprise me.*
>
> —BOB WEIR

Co-writing is standard practice in the commercial songwriting world, because it is an efficient way to crank out a lot of songs that maintain a high professional standard. The collaborative process also can lead to songs that are less idiosyncratic and personal than what one songwriter might write—and so may be more easily transferable to a recording artist.

> *I think good co-writing collaborations should be teaching and learning exchanges. I've written fifty songs with Allan Shamblin—well, Alan Shamblin's strong suit as a writer is imagery and very specific painting of*

pictures. There are not too many people who are better than him at that. When I started writing with him ten years ago, I was not nearly as adept at that as I am now, and he's part of the reason. And hopefully he would say that I taught him something, because I was always musically well versed and good at the big-picture chorus-lyric kind of thing.

You know, co-writing can be both fabulous and awful, depending on who you are doing it with. In order to find the ten or so soulmates that I now have that I write songs with all the time, I've probably written with over a hundred people and maybe written only one song with most of them. It doesn't mean that those experiences were terrible; it just means that the magic wasn't quite there or that we just didn't click on a certain level as people. And sometimes your writing styles just don't mesh, even two writers who really admire each other. But I think the only way to find those people you do click with is to try a lot of people.

—STEVE SESKIN

Co-writing is not only a chance to stretch and improve as a writer but a networking opportunity.

If two or three people are involved in a song, that song might have more legs in terms of getting other people to hear it. Maybe somebody would cut it.

It's beneficial in many ways, and it's good just to get off your butt and write. If you're going to be a writer, you have to write a lot of stuff. I probably throw away two-thirds of what I write in order to get to the third of the stuff that really moves me. So I've got to get up this morning and inspire myself to write something. How am I going to do that? Maybe I can call up my friend and say, "What are you doing?" and throw some ideas back and forth. Maybe that's the spark you need that day.

—JONATHAN BYRD

In a good co-writing relationship, both partners are respectful of each other's talents, and are open and honest with each other. Each one is ready to be a cheerleader if the other is on a roll, or to step in and take the lead if things are stalled. Just as when you are writing by yourself, it's vital in co-writing to silence your inner judge and lose your self-consciousness when you are brainstorming ideas together. Be ready to sing, say, or play anything, no matter how lame it may be, and give your partner the same freedom. Bad ideas often lead to great ideas.

Co-writers also need to be unconcerned with who takes credit for what. This process is about serving the song, not staking claims or feeding egos. In some long-term songwriting partnerships, the writers agree to split the credit equally for every song created—that's what Lennon and McCartney did with the Beatles, even though they wrote many songs individually with no input from the other. Brandi Carlile and her songwriting collaborators and bandmates Tim and Phil Hanseroth do the same thing with their collective song catalogue. By removing the question of individual credit from the equation, said Carlile, "There's no ego. The music wins and takes precedence."

> We don't get too precious about our songwriting. If one of us has an idea that's half done, nobody's going to get possessive because they want the credit for it. Nobody's going to get their feelings hurt by going, yeah, I want to write this one alone. We are all really open to just the song being the best.
>
> —Tim Hanseroth

In co-writing, assigning credit is a problematic exercise anyway. One writer may concentrate on the lyrical side while the other focuses on the music, but the lines between their contributions are often blurry, because they are each giving editorial feedback on the other's ideas. If one person writes almost all the lyrics but the other comes up with the best line, who is the most important lyricist? It's a great song; who cares?

The same philosophy applies to all the sundry ways we have talked about to beg, borrow, steal, coax, tease, and puzzle out your ideas as you are writing a song. If it's a great song, who cares how you got there? All you can do is try a lot of approaches and see what works for you. The measure of your success is right there in the song. Congratulations!

ONSTAGE

Songs these days fly instantly around the world in little packets of data, yet that dazzling display of technology never changes the fundamental equation of music: a performer, an audience, a song. Just as email doesn't replace a face-to-face conversation over coffee, recordings aren't the same as music communicated person to person.

Performing has a special value for a songwriter. The stage is where you see how your songs fare out in the world: you kiss them good-bye at the bus stop on their way to school, and later they come back to report on who teased them on the playground and who their new friends are. That's not an easy thing for every parent/songwriter to do, but that's how both you and your progeny learn and grow. In writing a song, you have taken your best shot at communicating a story or idea or emotion; putting it out there for an audience is one small test of where you have nailed it and where you haven't quite—not just as a writer, but as an instrumentalist and singer and raconteur. And that test, in combination with all the others conducted in different settings and with different groups of people, helps you set your agenda for improving your existing repertoire and writing the next batch of songs. For a songwriter, there is nothing more validating and thrilling than to witness one of your own creations connecting with a listener.

In the digital age, performing is more important than ever for building an audience and a career. It's fantastic that you can record tracks in your bedroom and share them worldwide, but how do you make anyone outside friends and family notice or care that you did so? The answer, for most

musicians, is still onstage and on the road, making your case audience by
audience, song by song. Sure, some artists do establish themselves purely
through recorded tracks and videos and social media, but more often than
not, success in the music marketplace is still functionally dependent on
your activities down on Mother Earth.

> *Kids come up to me, and they want advice about what's the magic formula
> to get the national tours and the distribution. You can see they want,
> want, want all these things. And I think, maybe you should just try to get
> a gig. Maybe you should just get a gig, and maybe you should do that
> every weekend for ten years, and then see if you're not on a haphazard
> national tour that grew organically and if you don't have some recordings
> that you made along the way that are distributed through the people you
> encountered along the way.*
>
> —ANI DIFRANCO

> *The more valuable thing is always going to be the more scarce thing. So
> when everybody's lives are led online, then having a great live performance
> is going to help you stand out from the pack so much more than being
> one of the one million musicians with a great Web presence a click away.*
>
> —DEREK SIVERS

There are, truth be told, plenty of things about gigging that can just
plain suck. The heroic effort made in exchange for barely enough money to
buy gas and a slice of pizza. The late night followed by the crack-of-dawn
start of your day job. The club bookers who never return your calls. The
sound guy who butchered your guitar tone. The people gabbing at the front
table. The not-all-that-funny-anymore requests for "Stairway" or "Free
Bird." The tedium of airports and budget motels, the significant others
miles away . . . As an emerging artist, you have to develop a thick skin and
a long-term perspective, and focus instead on the small things that do go
right: the four people who signed your mailing list, the woman who said
she loved the last song of the set and wanted it on CD, the couple you
recognized from a previous gig.

The circuit of established venues is nowhere near big enough to accommodate all the musicians who could successfully play them given

ANI DIFRANCO

decent promotional support. In some parts of the country and some styles of music, that circuit is practically nonexistent. Fortunately, that situation has inspired music lovers to create viable alternatives—off-the-beaten-track venues where performers might find a small but appreciative audience. The existence of these places means that no matter where you are, you can probably find somewhere to share your songs, either as a first step toward bigger venues or just as a satisfying outlet in and of itself.

Let's take a tour through today's performing scene, from stage craft to venues to gear to booking, and listen to words of wisdom from some well-traveled troubadours.

GETTING READY TO PERFORM

There are people who are born entertainers, gregarious types who love nothing more than putting on a show. But for most of us, it takes time and experience to feel confident as performers—in fact, those attracted to the self-contained creative world of the singer-songwriter tend to be intro-spective souls who are not at all in their natural element onstage. That's certainly true of me—I've always had to be nudged to perform, even though I'm secretly eager to do it—and many artists over the years have described to me their battles with stage fright. But even the shyest, most reserved singer-songwriters *can* become effective and even great performers, because they have a secret power: belief in their own songs. If it feels good and natural singing your songs in private, you can learn to tap into that feeling in front of an audience, too.

Success onstage begins with comfort in your own skin and with your own music. In performance, you don't act the same as you do hanging out at home—you are accentuating certain aspects of your personality and suppressing others. But the bottom line is that your identity as a performer is some version of yourself, and it has to come across as authentic to the audience. Even if you are taking a more theatrical approach and essentially inventing a stage persona, as David Bowie or Beck does, the character that you are inhabiting has to be someone you (like a good actor) can relate to and deliver with conviction—just as when you're writing a song in character, you have to identify with that character for the song to come alive.

Louise Taylor described the realization that helped her overcome her deep discomfort with making music in public.

It feels good now. It feels like I've come to who I am. I didn't understand that that's what an audience really wants. For a long time I thought they wanted something I imagined you had to be or you had to do, and very slowly I came around to the idea that really what the audience wants you to be is yourself—something that comes across as real.

—LOUISE TAYLOR

Nothing teaches you about performing more effectively and quickly than just doing it. You don't have to learn in front of a highly critical audience, either. There are many informal and supportive settings that can help you find your footing before you play on an actual stage (see the next section for ideas), and even when you do make that step, the indifferent audiences you are likely to encounter at first give you plenty of time and space to grow. So cut yourself some slack and consider each show another assignment for Gigging 101.

As with songwriting, there are no rules about how to perform successfully—you have to find a style of presentation that suits your personality, your music, your audience, and the venue. Here are some suggestions and observations on stage craft to help you along the way.

PRACTICE REALISTICALLY. The best way to prepare for any kind of show is to simulate as closely as possible how you will be playing. That means if you plan to stand onstage, practice that way at home. Set up microphones or an amp or whatever you're going to be using, so that you are accustomed to working with your gear. And go through your set from start to finish without taking a break for chips and salsa or tuning up for ten minutes. When you make a mistake, pretend that there is an audience waiting for you to get on with it (more on that below). If you can assemble a small test audience—your friend, partner, sibling, cat—all the better.

PRACTICE TALKING. You may feel a little silly doing it at home alone, but you can practice the talking as well as the playing. Musicians who are really good at rapping with the audience seem like they are being completely spontaneous, but in reality they are drawing on a repertoire of jokes, stories, and asides that they have developed over a long stretch of gigs.

It's just like improvising on an instrument; you are spontaneously recombining and extending all the little riffs and moves you've memorized over the years.

So think in advance about some things you might say during your set. If you are intimidated by the prospect of talking onstage, think small—don't expect or try to become a stand-up comedian overnight. Practice these little raps along with your songs at home, and then at the gig take note of what worked and what didn't, and store that information away for future use. It's a gradual process, finding a way of speaking that fits with your stage persona and your music. Many top-flight entertainers started out anxious and tongue-tied onstage.

> *When I started I didn't look up from the guitar neck, and I had to write out what I was going to say in between songs, even if it was "This next song's called . . ."*
>
> —PATTY LARKIN

> *My dad was really good at it. He was always the one who would tell stories and make up songs on the spot about audience members. We'd do the four hour-long sets, and we would walk around between sets and talk to everyone. I was really shy and stiff onstage, real self-conscious. And then I went through other phases where I'd been onstage so long, at age fourteen or fifteen, that it would get way* too *comfortable—you're too relaxed and you don't have any respect for it. You're not entertaining; you're just like in your living room.*
>
> *I think when I started playing my own music, I came into my own, because I get lost in the emotion of the song—I don't have to think about it at all. I just learned to have a rapport with the audience and talk and tell stories and joke around, and I began to enjoy that as much as singing.*
>
> —JEWEL

USE YOUR NERVES.   Most people consider the jitters they feel before going onstage to be an obstacle (I'm so nervous, how am I ever going to pull this off?) or a sign of inexperience (if I really knew what I was doing, I wouldn't be so nervous). But there's another way to look at those butterflies in the pit of your stomach: as a source of energy. Nervous energy is what helps you rise above your everyday self and deliver a great show. I have on many occasions chatted with artists both before and after a gig, and I'm amazed at how edgy even the most seasoned and seemingly natural performers are beforehand, and how they are almost like different people when they finally relax afterward. The fact that they still feel that edge before their umpteenth gig is one reason they are so good at what they do.

So think of your preshow nervousness as something that helps you get pumped up to play your best. And remember that the stage is a dynamic environment with a constant energy flow between you and your audience. Your nerves help to generate the musical energy that you send out into the room, and the audience reaction—which is what you are most nervous about—completes the cycle. Even strangers and just-happened-to-be-there listeners want you to succeed, for their own selfish reasons: they want to have a good time. You are in this together.

LIGHTEN UP. Your songs may be brooding and dark, but that doesn't mean you have to be that way during your whole set. A little self-deprecating joke or aside gives your listeners a necessary breather (there's a reason gallows humor exists) and shows that you don't take yourself too seriously. And lightening up for a moment may in fact heighten the impact of your next sad song.

EASE INTO IT. Kick off a performance with songs that are familiar and easy to play and help you get into the groove. Even if you have warmed up well beforehand (which you should do, both your voice and your hands), you need to settle in once your show starts, and so does your audience. If someone is mixing your sound, there's a good chance that he or she will be tweaking the mixing board during your first song, because a room with people in it sounds different from the empty room where you conducted your sound check. So save your tricky stuff and new stuff for later in the set.

PREPARE TO BE FLEXIBLE. A good set list offers well-thought-out variety in mood, tempo, key, and song length, but ideally you should be open to making on-the-spot adjustments. If you keep a few songs in reserve, perhaps jotted down to jog your memory, you'll be ready if you're asked to extend your set beyond what you were originally planning to play (if that happens, congratulations!) or—a more likely scenario—if you want to make substitutions based on how the set is going. If the crowd is not attentive, you might want to skip that subtle mood song and substitute something more direct and upbeat. Or people may respond with surprising enthusiasm to the oddball cover you sometimes play, so maybe it would be a good idea to throw in another along the same lines.

It all boils down to being a listener as well as a player onstage, paying attention to what is going on in the room and with your songs, as Jason Mraz once said while reflecting on his coffeehouse days.

If you find that the song you just played didn't really do it and everyone's yakking, then make up for it somehow in the story you're going to tell, and just basically create a relationship with your audience that isn't all about "look at me." It's all about "look at us": we're all here in this moment, and it's never going to happen this way again. So it was always a matter of staying present and having a sense of relatedness. I used humor and the awkward and embarrassing moments of my life to create that safe place for an audience to be comfortable and participate in these songs.

—JASON MRAZ

CATER YOUR MUSIC TO THE SETTING. The stage is a very different environment from the studio, and savvy performers exploit those differences.

I see them as quite separate entities and chances to do very different things with your music. There's a kind of energy you can put into that show that you can't do on a record—namely visuals. Just jumping up in the air and moving around and that kind of physical, visual energy adds so much to what you're doing, and you can't do that on a record. We do a lot of improv when we play live, making up songs and kind of hacking around, that wouldn't stand up with repeated listening. That's not what it's for. It's about the moment, about feeding off the audience, and it might not make sense to a person sitting there listening to a recording of it two months later who's not in the building, who's doesn't know what happened just before it. And similarly, on a record you can do things that are so subtle and so thought out that they would be lost in an arena. What we strive to do is to take advantage of both those things.

—ED ROBERTSON

Not only do you need to adapt your presentation to the live setting, you need to consider which songs are the best choices for your set list. There are songs (originals and covers) that would seem goofy on a record but are big winners onstage, as well as strong album tracks that somehow don't translate into performance pieces. Just keep trying things and see what works, and over time you will wind up with a live repertoire that overlaps but doesn't precisely match your album track lists.

DON'T APOLOGIZE.   So often I have heard performers apologize to the audience about the cold they have, their lack of finesse on their instrument, the likelihood they are going to make a mistake in the new song they are about to play . . . From the audience's perspective, these apologies are simply annoying—you're telling them in advance that you're not going to deliver as good a show as you should or could. Who wants to be told that? Just concentrate on doing your best given all the limitations and circumstances of that particular night. If you want to briefly explain that you're recovering from bronchitis and just getting your voice back, that's fine, but don't apologize for the fact that you have been sick. The audience will sympathize and root for you as you give it your best shot.

USE YOUR MISTAKES.   Everybody flubs a line or a chord sometime, and it is not a disaster. It's not like stumbling on your triple axel in Olympic figure skating competition, where you know that row of scowling judges just knocked your scores way down and you blew your chance for a medal. On the contrary, a mistake onstage can be an opportunity to bond with your audience if you laugh or shrug it off or play with it. The best performers transform mistakes into great moments: I've heard Martin Sexton, for instance, stop after a garbled line and do a dead-on imitation of a tape rewinding, completely cracking up the crowd. Your audience does not expect you to be superhuman and technically perfect, which is a pretty meaningless concept when it comes to music anyway.

> *I'm definitely not a perfectionist. It's after years of gigging, you get people coming up and saying, "Oh, my favorite bit was when you fucked up that song." That's the special bit no one else is going to get on another night, where you're human and where people can laugh.*
>
> —KT TUNSTALL

You can prepare yourself to deal with the inevitable glitches. As you practice your set at home, pretend you are in front of an audience and need to make an entertaining or at least smooth recovery from a mistake. Learn how to keep cruising past a small flub, which an audience will soon forget anyway. If it's a bigger mistake, like starting a song in the wrong key or singing the wrong first line of a verse, think about ways to acknowledge the mistake in a lighthearted way and then restart. If you mess up somewhere in the middle of a song, keep the rhythm going while you loop around to make the second attempt, so that you do not completely stop the flow. If you play guitar onstage, be ready to deal with the gremlins of out-of-tune and broken strings. Tuning and string-changing jokes are an entire subgenre of stage humor. I will always remember a fiery festival performance by the late Michael Hedges in which he broke a string and then pulled a spare out of a bag with an exaggerated sweep of his arm, as if he were a knight brandishing his sword for a duel. It was funny and dramatic—who knew grabbing an extra string could be a grandiloquent gesture?—and the crowd loved it.

> *There's something about walking onstage that makes you think you've got to be good, you'd better not be a disappointment, and you'd better not make a mistake. All of that is horseshit. None of it applies. The opposite is true: you will be a disappointment; you will make mistakes; you will have nights that are just empty at best. And be happy with them.*
>
> *There's something automatically there when you walk on, by contract. It's what "in concert" means. I think it starts before anybody is in the building. It's something about people knowing that they're going to meet*

as strangers or otherwise in a room and share this musical experience.
You walk out and the motor's running, and what you do is just follow
that. That's what's doing the work. It's really delusional to think you are
what's happening, because you're not. You are kind of the excuse, maybe
the focal point, or more accurately maybe the trigger. What's really going
on is just that curve, and if you pay attention to that, boy, it's the most
fun on earth.

—LEO KOTTKE

RESPECT THE AUDIENCE. Let's face it: people who are sitting and listening to
you play music on any given night have plenty of other things they could
be doing. They're giving you their time and perhaps their money, and you
need to respect that. You are offering them the gift of your music, but no
one appreciates a gift that's sullenly dropped at their feet.

I think I used to feel angry at the audience for looking at me, because I
was very shy and not very comfortable with myself. And I've learned that
you can't do that; if someone is looking at you, if they've paid money to
see you, then you'd better put on a show and not sit there and be morose.

—SUZANNE VEGA

Respecting the audience doesn't mean you have to be all saccharine
smiles and gee-whiz appreciation. There's a long tradition of taking a pro-
vocative or confrontational stance with the audience, and that can be very
effective in the right setting. But even being aggressive is a form of respecting the audience: it's an acknowledgment that you need to do more
sometimes than just play the song, a way of pushing people and starting
the cycle of action and reaction that drives a great show.

At times you will encounter audience members who are unforgivably
rude, interrupting you or otherwise spoiling the atmosphere. It's never
easy, but try not to take these things personally. Rise above it. You have
more important things to do than spar with some schmuck who's trying to
get attention. Ignoring him might be the best way to silence him anyway.

You can play with a 104-degree fever and your heart fibrillating, but you
can't play if you are infuriated. If something is really blowing your stack,

Suzanne Vega

you've got to drop that as quickly as possible, because that's the one emo-
tion that can screw it all up for you.

—Leo Kottke

Acknowledge where you are.   Audiences like to have the feeling that they are
part of a unique evening and not just watching a performer do the same
show she did last night and the night before and 120 other times this year.

Think about ways in which you can acknowledge that you are standing on that particular stage in that particular town on that particular night. It doesn't have to be pumping your arms and shouting, "How ya doin', Schwenksville!" It could be as small a thing as thanking the headliner or mentioning someplace you went earlier that day. Such personal details are part of the reason people are there listening to you rather than cocooning with onscreen entertainment at home.

SHOW THEM IN. Playing original songs for people who don't know them is a challenging gig. It requires a lot more of your audience than if you were singing pop covers or pounding out formulaic bar-band blues. So think about how you can draw people into the world of your songs. Imagine that your song is a new friend from out of town, and you are bringing him to a party and introducing him around. What might you say? Maybe something about how he grew up on a llama ranch, or about his job as a food stylist, or about how you two met while chaining yourself to a redwood tree in California—whatever you think will be an intriguing detail that will lead to further conversation. Your song introductions can perform a similar function. You don't want to bore people with too much trivia (or too much talking in general), but a well-chosen anecdote or two can help them get to know you and your songs a little bit better.

And even if your focus is on original songs, don't rule out playing covers, by the way, especially if you can find a unique slant on a familiar song that makes it feel like yours. In your set, a cover gives listeners a break from the new and unfamiliar and freshens their ears for the next original song. Plus, your taste in covers reveals something about where you are coming from musically and, in turn, helps illuminate why you write the kinds of songs you write.

KEEP IT MOVING. Try to minimize the lag time between songs. If you need to retune, move the capo, or switch instruments, learn to do so quickly and efficiently; start making the change while people are applauding after the last song, and if you're still at it when the room quiets down, talk to the audience over the gap if you can. (You can reduce the number of these transitions when making your set list, too, by grouping songs in the same tuning or on the same instrument.) Introduce songs when you've got something worthwhile to say, but for other songs, just jump in with no introduction. Long pauses can become really awkward and sap the energy of a show.

STAY IN THE POCKET.   Performing is an adrenaline rush, and that can easily lead to breakneck tempos. It's thrilling to go fast and feel the wind in your hair, but be careful not to kick off a song at an unsustainable tempo or accelerate to the point that you can't sing the words or play the riff properly. Before you start, hear the ideal groove in your head for a few seconds so you nail it right from the downbeat.

WORK THE MIC.   Back in high school, I remember listening back to sound-board tapes of my band and wondering for a few disorienting moments who the hell that singer was with the froggy voice. Yup, it was me—I was so amped up by being onstage in front of all those dancing classmates that my voice kept rising into this half yell that completely changed its timbre in a pretty unflattering way. In other words, I wasn't making good use of the microphone pointed at my mouth.

For a singer, a microphone is a great thing: it allows you to whisper and shout and all points in between. So use the mic; it's your friend. And don't be afraid to get right on it, which boosts the low end in your voice and makes you sound big even when you bring it down to a soft hum.

USE DYNAMICS.   In a setting where you are competing for people's attention, dynamics are one of your best tools. Contrast is the key. Build to a loud climax and then stop abruptly. Do a live fade-out. And if the chatter is starting to drown you out, try bringing your volume way down rather than up. People have become so used to shouted conversations in the back of rock clubs that they are unlikely to surrender if you try to be louder than they are.

When you turn down, it seems that people listen harder. A lot of people's volume approach is to turn the electric guitar up to twelve and people won't be able to help but listen, but our approach has kind of been the softer we are, the more acoustic we are, people will lean in and listen a little bit more.

—LAURA LOVE

VARY THE ACCOMPANIMENT. When you are performing solo, your voice and your words may be the focus of attention, but your instrument is a lot of what the audience will be hearing. So work hard on giving your songs distinctive and varied accompaniment parts.

You can accomplish this goal without becoming a virtuoso player. If you're a guitar strummer, learn to fingerpick a little. Switch instruments for a song or two; all you really have to know how to do on the other instrument is play that song or two. Sing over hand percussion or a cappella—the unaccompanied voice is always arresting. These kinds of change-ups are so refreshing in the middle of a long stream of songs played on the same instrument.

GET YOUR GEAR IN ORDER. We will cover this subject in more detail below, but the last thing you want during a performance is to be worrying about your gear. Keep it simple and functional and as close to trouble free as you can manage. Use your gear at home so there are no nasty surprises at the gig. If you will be using a house sound system, microphone, and other equipment, be sure you know exactly what will be available and that your own gear will be compatible with it. Develop a routine for setting up everything you need (or might need) and then tuning your instruments, and follow it religiously before every show.

WORK WITH YOUR HOSTS. The people who book shows, tend bar, wait tables, run sound, work the door, and handle other roles at the venue won't always treat you as cordially and respectfully as you would hope. But the fact is, they are hosting you. You are providing a service to them, and they are providing a service to you. All of your jobs are a lot of work for not a lot of pay. So no matter how you feel you are being (mis)treated, be a pro: Show up on time, be friendly with your hosts and any other musicians on the bill, learn their names, and (yes, this is your mother speaking) say please and thank you. Make a point of thanking them by name onstage, too. Not only will this make your evening more pleasant, but it might win over some allies and lead to more gigs there or elsewhere down the road.

BUILD YOUR LIST.   At every gig, no matter how small, have a place where new fans can sign up on an email list. Be sure you get their zip codes at least so you can target your announcements to those who live near where you're playing (no sense telling the folks in Tampa about your gig in Buffalo). A good mailing list is an essential promotional tool for an independent artist.

If you've got CDs to sell, you should have at least a few on hand. Going home with your disc might make the difference between "Oh yeah, that woman was good—what was her name again?" and a diehard fan, and you may make more at the merch table than you do from the door. Flyers that announce upcoming events and point people to your website are a good idea too. You may not need all this stuff each time, but it's a lost opportunity if some new fans ask about your CDs and all you can do is tell them to look you up online.

TAKE THE LONG VIEW.   If there's a common theme to all this advice, it is to be patient. As much as we all dream about the rocket ride to the stars, most long-term careers in music are built one fan at a time. It takes time to find your groove as a performer and to find the people who respond to what you have to say. No single gig is definitive; each is a step in an ongoing process of developing and learning and sharing.

Remember, too, that there are many varieties of performing musicians. There are those with day jobs who long to devote their lives to music, and those who perform occasionally without any professional aspirations. There are the local heroes who teach and gig only in their hometown, the regional acts who stay within a radius of a hundred miles, and those seemingly full-time pros who tour nationally but actually pay their bills with a flexible job during stints at home. No matter how you make a living, don't confuse the financial status of your music with its inherent value as art. The moment you get up in front of people to play music, it doesn't matter if you've spent your day doing data entry or teaching fifth graders or polishing your Grammy awards: what counts is the passion and sweat you put into your songs.

And whatever your disappointments and successes in the performing world, remember that when you step onstage and play your songs, you are offering something that no one else can offer: your music and a view of the world from where you (and only you) stand. That is a priceless gift.

FINDING VENUES

In the performing scene today, much more is going on than meets the eye when you browse the local entertainment listings. There are the established venues, from arenas on down through theaters and clubs and coffee-houses, but if you dig a little deeper you will also find musical happenings in backyards, church basements, and many other unexpected places. For a developing artist, these informal settings are an excellent place to gain experience in front of a sympathetic audience.

Before you even step onto something resembling a stage, though, you can find opportunities for sharing your songs. Start right at your own house—just ask friends or family if they'd like to hear a new song or two. If you feel awkward making the suggestion, drop a large hint by leaving your instrument out in the living room. If you know some local musicians, organize a jam session (collective playing on familiar songs) or a song circle (swapping original and off-the-beaten-track songs). Keep an ear out for these kinds of gatherings in your community. Aside from private parties, such get-togethers might be organized through a local folk society, music store, or church. In warm weather, they may happen at the farmers' market or street fair. Ask around—you might be surprised at what goes on right under your nose.

Summer festivals are a fantastic place to play, as well as listen to, music. Festivals with a lot of campers often have jam sessions that extend through the night, and at some events (like the Kerrville Folk Festival in Texas) the campfire scene rivals the main stage as an attraction. Each circle tends to have a particular orientation: fiddle tunes, Grateful Dead songs, blues and swing, originals . . . Grab your instrument and scout around for a gathering that best suits what you do, then find a place in the circle. Remember that sharing is a two-way street, though. It's obnoxious to cut in so you can play your song as soon as possible and then take off to find your next slot. Listen and learn. Join in if it seems appropriate, but let each player have his or her moment.

When it comes to locating actual performance venues, look up the itineraries of artists who do something similar to what you do or are aspiring to do. You will quickly see that on the lower rungs of the music-business ladder, active performers are playing at all kinds of places other than clubs and coffeehouses. Such as . . .

OPEN MICS.   Open mics fill an important role as places where anyone can get up and play a few songs on a real stage, sound system and all. Playing at an open mic is worthwhile not just for logging stage time but for making connections with your local music community, since most of the audience consists of other musicians. Many artists have started this way, building from open mics to pass-the-hat sets to actual paying gigs, and even experienced pros show up at open mics to test out new material or just because they want to *play*. When I first moved to the San Francisco area from the East Coast, open mics helped me get my bearings and meet other musicians—including some well-established performers who hosted these events—and led to a monthly gig at one venue.

Many coffeehouses and clubs host open mics, usually on a slow night early in the week. Some are specifically designed as songwriter showcases, and they might include feedback on your presentation and material. I've participated in open mics run by songwriters' associations that even include written feedback from guest judges. The open mics and writers' nights hosted by Nashville's tiny Bluebird Café have made it a mecca for songwriters.

The sign-up routines for open mics vary from place to place. Patience is required, because there may be a lottery in which you show up early to pick a time slot that may end up being hours later. If you hope that your fellow performers are going to hang around and listen to you, then hang around and listen to them as well—an educational experience in its own right.

You learn a lot more from seeing open mics than you do from seeing polished shows. You just watch what works and what doesn't.

—DAVID WILCOX

For more experienced performers, hosting an open mic can be a good (modestly) paying gig. Some open mic nights also include a longer feature slot that is booked by the host, which is a stepping stone to full-length shows of your own.

SCHOOLS.   When my kids were small, I had a blast taking my guitar into preschools and elementary schools to sing songs for and with kids. Kids (especially young ones) are about as responsive an audience as you'll ever get. When they like something, they beam and clap and groove, and when they're bored, they fidget and look around for something better to do. They learn songs amazingly fast, and they teach some valuable lessons about songwriting—especially the power of simple expression and the singable melody. They also can be very easily brought into the songwriting process, and making up a song in collaboration with kids (from a familiar melody or from scratch) is an educational and entertaining experience all around.

If you are looking to volunteer your services in a school, all you really have to do is ask—teachers often welcome the opportunity to bring special activities like this into the classroom. Paid performances are set up either by an individual school (arranged by a teacher, administrator, or the PTA) or through a central agency; call the school to find out how it works. Compared to regular venues, said veteran school performer Walkin' Jim Stoltz, school gigs are "much more laid back. I don't have to worry about the promotion, and booking is generally much, much easier. Folks will return your calls from a school." You will probably have to bring your own equipment to a formal performance, because the gymnasium isn't, after all, a concert hall.

> I think it is very important that performers want to be there for motives beyond money. You have to like kids and enjoy being around them. And you need to have a show that is educational in some way. Most schools want more than just music. They want a theme to the performance that is going to enhance the educational experience of their students. My show has simple environmental lessons but also has ties to science, geography, music, and writing. A teacher can easily use my show to build on a number of subjects and lessons.

*My advice to any musicians looking into doing school concerts is to
have fun. Teach, but have fun. Talk to the kids as you would to anyone.
Don't talk down to them. Keep them involved with what you are doing.
Let them participate in the show. Every song I perform is a sing-along,
squeak-along, or howl-along. Tell them stories about yourself. The sooner
they get to know you, the more successful you will be in getting your
message across. Try to have a question-and-answer time after the show
with some of the classes. Again, the kids will get to know you better and
appreciate what you do much more. When the kids appreciate you, the
teachers do too.*

—WALKIN' JIM STOLTZ

SENIOR CENTERS AND OTHER INSTITUTIONS.   Wherever you live you'll find opportunities to bring music to places where people can't get out to hear it, such as
senior centers, hospitals, shelters, and prisons. They may not be your typical
listeners, but they will surely appreciate your presence. Performing in an
institutional setting for people who are hungry for art and diversion can
be a very moving experience.

By calling around you may find paying gigs in places like senior centers,
or you can volunteer to play. Some cities have organizations that set up
these performances; in the San Francisco area, for instance, Bread and
Roses has been providing this service since the '70s.

BUSKING.   Then there is always the sidewalk, the subway station, the pedes-
trian mall, or the public square—playing for tips in a kind of performance
boot-camp environment. Busking is not for shrinking violets, but it can be
lucrative and very good for your chops. Woody Pines, who played daily for
several years on the streets of New Orleans' French Quarter, described
some of the most useful lessons of busking.

*You learn when you need an upbeat song, and then you learn actually
you can suck them in by playing a slow song. You learn to project and
play with a little bit more energy that gets that nice, authentic sound with
strings buzzing on frets—really trying to get your instrument out there,
competing with a garbage truck and a parade that goes by, the blues band*

on the other block. You don't necessarily need to scream and shout, but then a few hollers don't hurt.

—WOODY PINES

Peter Mulvey, who forged his style on the streets of Dublin and the subway stations of Boston (and later recorded an album on his customary subway bench), cited a number of benefits of busking aside from the change collected: It focuses you on the essentials—the melody and the groove. Since nobody is going to pretend to be interested in what you're doing, it provides tangible and immediate feedback; if you reach somebody (and they reach for their wallet), that's a real achievement. Busking is a good way to build a fan base of locals who might never hear you otherwise. And if you combine daytime busking with evening gigs, when you reach the stage you are warmed up and, in Mulvey's words, "humming like a cable."

Just by repetition, eventually you come to those peak moments when you really break through the ice and you are underwater—you're in the song. Whatever the tools you are using, that's the target you're shooting for in performance. And the subway was the first place I learned to do it. Some of the tools that you use in the subway are spontaneity and, actually, frustration. The trains coming and taking away your audience . . . it wears you down to a point of surrender, and sometimes that point of surrender gets you into the song. In a bizarre way, sometimes being locked out of it gets you into it.

—PETER MULVEY

If you think that busking might be for you, you've got to do a little preparation before hitting the street. You may need a permit, which you get from the town/city for free or a small fee, and you need to suss out local regulations about where, what, and how you can play. Unless you can cut through the ambient noise unplugged, you will have to assemble some sort of portable amplification rig (microphone, battery-powered amp, and so on). And, of course, you have to adapt your repertoire to the rough-and-tumble setting, focusing on songs that will carry over the din of horns and trains and conversations.

MUSIC STORES.   One retail space that is sometimes converted into a performance space is the music store—move those racks of songbooks and guitars out of the way, set up a PA and some chairs, and voilà. This is more likely to happen at a larger shop that doubles as a community music center, with classes, clinics, and jam sessions complementing the retail and repair business. Performances at a music store are often an offshoot of the educational program, featuring regular teachers or visiting clinicians who are sponsored by a manufacturer or publisher. Stop in and find out what's going on at your local music emporium.

Even for musicians not interested in developing a full teaching practice, by the way, it's a big asset to be able to conduct workshops on the side (instrumental technique, stage craft, songwriting, whatever your strength). Workshops help fill in spaces during tours, give you something productive to do in the afternoons, and open the door to concert appearances. In the summertime, many road warriors enjoy teaching for a week or two at one of the scores of music camps that happen all across the country, where kids and grown-ups alike come to live and breathe music all hours of the day. Many camps offer programs for songwriters, with classes and critiques led by active troubadours.

OPENERS.   Opening someone else's show is both a tremendous opportunity and a daunting challenge. You are in a high-profile club, with a lavish sound system and a real backstage. The room is packed and the audience is eager . . . for the headliner to play. From the point of view of the club, the opener's job is to warm up the crowd and extend the entertainment beyond the main attraction. From the opener's point of view, this is a chance to step up to the mic and make an impression on a room full of strangers. On the one hand, there's less pressure on the opener because it is really the headliner's night; on the other, there's more pressure because it is someone else's crowd. "Headliners must fill our niche and have the potential to fill the room," said Griff Luneberg, who for years booked Austin's Cactus Café. "Opening acts only need to be talented."

The reason to pursue opening slots is not for the money, which is minimal, but for the exposure. You are supporting the headliner in order to support your own efforts to be the headliner on a different night. That means, according to Jim Fleming of Fleming Artists, you should have a follow-up plan: a gig of your own within the next three or four months in the same city (preferably announced by flyers at the merch table), so anyone pleasantly surprised by your opening set can come and experience your full show. That's how you turn the interested listener into a fan.

Some performers who open shows feel like they want to show all the variety of what they do, and that's not necessarily the place to do it. If you're playing for only twenty or thirty minutes, you should just go out and knock their socks off, because what you want them to do is remember you. It's not the time to do three ballads or show off your fancy musicianship. Do the rest of it later, when you get your forty-five minutes or an hour or two sets.

—Jim Fleming

As a performer, you need to play these types of shows to learn how to play a big room. How does your show translate from thirty people to three thousand? There are differences, and you have to try it a couple times to get the hang of it. The first times I played in front of fanatical audiences, I worried, "Is my sound big enough? Can I hold their attention?" I came to the conclusion that if my songs and the way I performed them solo couldn't make a room of music fanatics be quiet and listen, I was in the wrong business. Nine times out of ten this has worked for me.

Most of the time these big shows allow you to meet and spend time with an artist who in many ways is your peer but has more experience and draws a hell of a lot more. There aren't too many ways in the modern music business to have a real mentor relationship; opening shows is one of the few.

—Erin McKeown

In this supporting role, your professionalism is extremely important. Arrive on time, be courteous to the headliner and the people at the venue, keep a low profile, be quick and efficient in setting up and taking down your gear, and above all, don't play longer than you're supposed to.

For opening acts, the cardinal sin is going over your allotted time. If it's thirty or forty minutes, be sure you do not go over. Headliners hate it, club bookers hate it, and you may not get booked again. Remember the audience did not pay to see you. Keep it short and sweet.

—GRIFF LUNEBERG

If at the end of your opening set the crowd is dying to hear more, congrats—you have done a bang-up job. Now go out and schmooze with your new admirers, and encourage them to take home your CD and come see you at your own show next month.

Opening slots are booked in different ways. Often the promoter suggests an opening act but needs approval from the headliner, so in this case, a relationship with the venue is what lands the gig. A headliner might request a specific opening act or bring him/her along on the road, but this is relatively rare in the singer-songwriter world outside of big names and big halls. Since the headliner is always involved one way or another in the selection of the opening act, networking with other compatible artists helps to bring these gigs your way.

It is possible to focus too much on openers and not enough on your own shows. At some point, Jim Fleming said, it's better to play your own show for two hundred people than it is to serenade two thousand people while they are buying beer and taking their seats for the main attraction. Look at openers as a way to poke your head into a higher level of the music business than where you are currently standing. With time and work, you may get to that place where yours is the big name on the marquee and someone else is supporting you.

ONLINE.   Online concerts have emerged as an important avenue for live music, allowing you to perform at home or wherever you are—and make money doing it.

It's easy to set up a live stream of a regular concert you're playing, as a way to reach some more folks and bring in a little extra revenue beyond what you earn at the door. But the more interesting use of the technology is performing an online-only show through a laptop or smartphone. Without an audience in the room, you can focus on playing for the camera and interacting with your online viewers. The ability for fans to chat with each other and with you is a big part of what makes online concerts special.

The chat function keeps it pretty interactive, so their feedback gets heard and I can take requests. They also talk to each other a lot. The audience knows each other by now, and I think they like being able to talk during a song and not get shushed.

—GLEN PHILLIPS

No doubt the technology will continue to change rapidly, but at this writing here's how online shows work. Setting up a show is free on one of the major online concert sites (see completesingersongwriter.com for links), which take a portion of whatever comes in from tickets and tips. You choose the ticket price. A good strategy is to make the show free or pay what you want, and then offer rewards—album downloads, posters, guitar lessons, or whatever else—for generous tipping.

Allow at least a few weeks to promote your show by sharing the link with friends/fans and all those far-flung people who never get a chance to hear you play live. Though some viewers may happen upon your show, your own contacts are more likely to draw an audience. Think about ways to give your online show a unique spin—for instance with a theme, an unusual location, or a special guest.

Performing online takes some getting used to. The silence at the end of a song feels weird at first, even if someone types "clap clap clap." In addressing the audience, bear in mind there can be a significant lag time— so if you ask people a question, by the time you see responses you have moved onto something else. You won't be able to banter with the audience as you can at the coffeehouse. Also, don't let reading the screen distract you from your first priority: playing your best. Some performers make a point of not reading the chat until the music is over.

Keep your show short—thirty to sixty minutes is typical. Finally, plan out your set but be flexible, and embrace the informality of being offstage.

It's strange singing into a laptop, but I find if I'm honest about that awkwardness, the audience appreciates it. The favorite moments tend to be the accidental ones. People love it when my dog starts howling or if my daughter comes in and sings a song.

—GLEN PHILLIPS

HOUSE CONCERTS.   For grassroots artists and listeners alike, house concerts are one of the brightest opportunities on the performing scene. Filling the voids left by regular venues, house concerts are hosted by music fans who turn their living rooms or basements or barns or whatever spaces into temporary music halls. A house concert is like a cross between a private party and a public event: the show is typically publicized through friends and friends of friends, with limited seating by advance reservation only and a suggested donation that goes mostly or entirely to the performer. Except for the larger and more established house concert series, there's no sound system or stage (in fact, be careful you don't stomp on the toes of people in the front row), and people often bring food and drink to share. So it's a literally homey event, with very close contact between the performer and the audience as well as between the performer and the host, who may offer the guest room and a meal as part of the package.

I've hosted and played lots of house concerts, and they have some qualities unlike any other shows. For one, the audience may know little or nothing about the performer or even the style of music that they're going to hear—they come because their friend invited them or just because the concept is novel and intriguing.

> *These are all people who know each other, but most of them don't know me, which is exciting. It's pretty special if the first time you hear me is in that setting. I really dig that aspect of it.*
>
> —SEAN ROWE

At a house concert, the audience may not be familiar with your music, but they are most definitely there to listen, and you could hear a pin drop in the room. So this is a chance to reach listeners who rarely set foot in clubs but are excited by the prospect of discovering good music in a unique setting. In many ways, it's an ideal situation for a singer-songwriter: for once, nobody is expecting you to supply background music or be a jukebox for their old favorites.

> *You sing one of your funny lines in your song, and everyone laughs because everyone heard it. You get to be in your element and deliver it*

how you intended it, without trying to win people over. You're playing for
an audience that's already won over because of the environment.

—KC Turner

The distraction-free atmosphere of a house concert is great for polishing
your craft, said singer-songwriter Fran Snyder, founder of the booking
network Concerts in Your Home.

There's an opportunity that's lost when you're playing for an inattentive
crowd: you don't really learn if your material is good or not. You can't get
the sort of detailed feedback that you get when you're playing up close and
personal in a room where the audience is not in darkness. As a developing
artist, I think that's critical, especially if you're doing understated material.

—Fran Snyder

Not every musician is cut out for the house concert environment. It
can be unnerving to have people listening so intently, at such close range,
if you're not used to it. And you also need to be prepared to interact with
the audience all night—before, during, and after your sets.

Socializing with your hosts is important, too—that's part of what moti-
vates them to do all the work of promoting the event, managing RSVPs,
moving furniture, preparing food, and opening their home to dozens of
people.

House concert hosts don't just love music—they love artists. And one of
the big reasons they put in the effort to host shows is not just for the music
but for the hang. It's for spending some time with these troubadours who
have great stories and great experiences to share and sort of a unique view
on life. All of that is lost if you have a performer who is not comfortable
or gregarious or happy to be around people.

—Fran Snyder

The financial arrangements for house concerts vary, but they are often
a sweet deal for the artist compared with playing at a club: you get all (or
most) of the donations, plus CD sales and perhaps free room and board for
a night. So you might carry away more money from playing a house concert
for twenty people than you would playing for three times that many people

in a club, and the host probably did most of the legwork of publicizing the show. Unlike clubs that present show after show, week after week, a house concert is a special event for the host and will be treated as such.

These days, house concerts happen all over and have become an underground circuit, especially in the folk world. The Web is the best place to locate existing series and learn more about how house concerts operate (see completesingersongwriter.com), but keep in mind that any fan is a potential host. You could suggest that possibility the next time someone says, "Why don't you ever play in my town?"

As you look into playing house concerts, remember that the hosts are volunteering their time and their homes because they love the music; this is not "just business" to them. Although you want to be clear about the arrangement, you should treat your hosts a little differently than you would the presenters at a commercial venue. You might, for instance, normally ask for a guarantee, but you shouldn't expect house concert hosts to make that commitment. Chances are, the host is going to work very hard to fill the room and create a successful evening all around.

GEAR MATTERS

My whole life is the way that guitar sounds coming back through the monitors.

—ANI DIFRANCO

There are basically two kinds of musicians: those who obsess over their gear, and those who can't remember the model numbers of their instruments to save their lives. While the former are constantly scouting out new gear and hotly debating their preferences with fellow gearheads, the latter are asking, "Is this thing on?" In my years as a music journalist, I've spent quite a bit of time trying to ferret out the details of what equipment performers are using and why, and my questions are greeted as often with a slightly embarrassed shrug as by a lengthy dissertation on the merits of one gizmo over another.

In my early twenties I went out with a guy who had thirteen different guitars, and he used to sit and explain to me the differences among them and what work he had done on which one on that particular day and how he had done this and that to the humbucker and switched a pickup here and there. . . . Once I literally fell asleep while he was talking to me. I thought it was funny when I woke up, but he was not amused.

—Suzanne Vega

Just as encyclopedic knowledge of music theory doesn't in itself lead to good songwriting, there is no correlation between being a gear expert and being a great player. It's the ideas, not the tools, that count. But the fact is, even if you don't understand or think much about gear, you still need to use it to make and share music. In performance, your equipment directly affects how you feel and what people hear.

It's important to have a great sound. We're picky, picky—I mean I can hear a string imbalance in the middle of a crowded bar. It's important to me. And it's not a reflection of being a good player, 'cause I'm not even a good player. The guitar has to be an extension of you in order to perform with it, so it's got to sound great. It can sound great in a crappy bar or a big room. It's not about having the most expensive equipment; it's just that your guitar has to feel like you.

—Amy Ray

When it comes to equipment, there are endless permutations in taste, sophistication, and budget. Obviously the gear considerations are different if you have a crew setting up your Wall of Sound in arenas across the land (hi, Bono!). But for singer-songwriters schlepping themselves and their gear from gig to gig, there are some rules of thumb.

KEEP IT SIMPLE. That is, keep your rig as simple as it can be while still delivering what you need it to deliver. Notice that I said *need* and not *want*. With music gear as with any consumer product, it's tricky to distinguish between what is essential and what is just shiny and new and has cool flashing lights, but that's what you have to do. The more you can strip down your rig, the less you have to carry, the quicker the setup, and the lower the odds that something will go wrong. And that all translates into more time for you to concentrate on the music.

Anytime you are thinking about upgrading your equipment, you need to consider the trade-off between sonic improvement and added complexity. If that new black box sounds better than your old black box but requires a lot more tweaking during every sound check, does the result justify the time and effort? Will the audience notice the difference? Will you?

Hand in hand with simplicity is reliability. There's nothing worse than dealing with a piece of equipment that is rattling, buzzing, or failing to emit any sound at a time when you should be mentally preparing for the show you're about to play. So invest a little more for gear that's rugged and reliable, just for the peace of mind. But more expensive isn't necessarily better. Stay away from stuff that sounds great but is finicky and fragile—there are a lot of amazing instruments, microphones, and other musical tools that are used widely in the studio but never onstage (and there's a very good reason why the cheap and nearly indestructible Shure SM57 and SM58 mics are found nearly everywhere music is amplified). It's just a matter of time before a piece of performing gear is dinged, dropped, or spilled on.

LEAVE YOUR PRECIOUS STUFF AT HOME.   No matter what instrument or equipment you're toting along to a performance, you have to be prepared for the possibility that it will get lost, stolen, damaged, or ruined. Sorry. The sad truth is that there are thieves, baggage handlers, and even careless friends out in the world who don't have the kinds of personal attachments to your gear that you do. So look at everything you are planning to bring with you and ask yourself the heart-wrenching question, "Can I afford to lose this, psychologically and financially?" If the answer is no, leave it at home. That may mean performing with your not-quite-favorite instrument and pretty good mic, but you will feel less stressed when you travel and more relaxed at the gig. As with all gear matters, you are making a compromise between what inspires you to play your best and what is most suited to the life of hard knocks. If you feel you've got to perform with an instrument of great cash or personal value, go for it—but make that decision with your eyes open.

If your instrument and expensive gear are properly insured, that may change the equation of what you feel comfortable bringing with you. Your homeowner's or renter's insurance might cover your instrument for damage or loss (double-check the details), but *not* if you are using it professionally. So a working musician needs special insurance coverage, which you may be able to obtain through membership in a musician's union or performing rights society like ASCAP and BMI.

MAKE A GIG PACK. Even the simplest instrument setup requires an assortment of additional gizmos and spare parts. So assemble a compact kit of all the things you might need and, whenever possible, extras: the list might include guitar accessories (strings, string winder, string cutter, picks, capo, nail file), electronic tuner, microphone (and perhaps a windscreen for a vocal mic), DI box, cables, batteries (for preamps, microphones, tuners, and so on), and maybe a few small repair items for your instrument if you are the tinkering sort. Get in the habit of bringing this pack along even if you're just going to the local coffeehouse, and then keeping it within easy reach while you play. It's better to be a little over-prepared than to be frantically searching for a new nine-volt battery right before a gig.

REDUCE THE VARIABLES. When you line up a show, check what gear will be available at the venue—and prepare for the possibility that it won't actually be there, or that it will be decrepit or dysfunctional. Consider bringing along one or two key items, such as a vocal microphone or a DI box, even if the venue supplies them. That'll make your setup and sound more consistent and—I'm sounding like a broken record here—allow you to focus more on the music and interacting with the audience.

MAINTAIN YOUR INSTRUMENT. Like cars and teeth, musical instruments need regular maintenance to function at their best. They aren't static objects but are constantly changed by the forces of time, string tension, playing, travel, weather, and the seasons. An annual setup on a guitar (or any fretted instrument), for instance, will make it easier and smoother to play, fix any buzzes and rattles, improve the tone and intonation, decrease string breakage, and generally catch small problems before they develop into big problems. That's a minor investment well worth making.

LISTEN TO YOUR PLUGGED-IN TONE. No matter how lovely your instrument sounds when you play it at home, what the audience hears is whatever comes out of the speakers—and for acoustic instruments, that sound is largely determined by your amplification rig. Too many singer-songwriters wind up with a rubber-band-y tone from their acoustic guitar pickups. You might get away with that in a band, where only a small part of your instrument's tone is cutting through the mix, but in a solo show, it's critical to have a full, pleasing sound.

Amplification systems for acoustic instruments have evolved to the point that you can get a good sound without blowing your bank account, carrying a ton of gear, or having an endless sound check—and a cheap instrument with the right pickup system can sound as good or better than a boutique beauty. Also, don't overlook the old-fashioned external microphone: when skillfully used in low-volume settings (especially without drums), an inexpensive mic can deliver an excellent approximation of what the instrument sounds like unplugged.

ASK OTHER MUSICIANS. By far the best source of information and advice about gear is other musicians who have been there, tried that. You won't have to pry—many performers love talking about this stuff and spend hours offstage trading tips and war stories. Gear preferences are subjective, of course, but at least you are listening to the voices of experience rather than the breathless hyperbole of some company's marketing department.

Other sources of gear advice include musicians' publications, which bring journalistic balance to how-to articles and reviews (and, for better or worse, a more diplomatic tone than what you'll hear in the green room), and online forums and reviews, where strangers sitting at keyboards around the world will tell you exactly what you should or should not buy. Since you know nothing about the real lives or hidden agendas of people posting online, give more weight to widely recurring recommendations than to any individual's foaming-at-the-mouth opinions.

FIND A GEAR GURU. If you just don't have that gear-obsession gene in you, cultivate a relationship with someone who does. This might be a repairer at the local music store or a fellow player—anyone who understands your needs, style, taste, and budget and can steer you toward the equipment that's the best match.

Music stores these days are packed with good products in all price ranges, as manufacturers have found ways to bring all sorts of high-end gear (for instance, guitars, microphones, and recording gear) into the reach of musicians on tight budgets. So the challenge isn't so much finding the good stuff as sorting through many, many options, and that's where reliable advice—from other musicians, a shop, a magazine, or wherever—is so valuable.

BOOKING BASICS

You love the writing. You're fascinated by the process of trying to capture your songs on record. You get a big buzz out of performing, and the good nights more than make up for the bad ones. But the booking? You will be hard pressed to find anyone who likes this part of being a working musician—booking is tough, frustrating work, with a lot of slings and arrows to endure for every success.

Booking also happens to be a necessary step if you are ever going to take the stage with your name by the door. And when you're starting out, you really don't have any choice but to buckle down and do it yourself. You may not have any idea what you're doing at first, but you fill all the other job requirements: You know your music better than anyone, and you are its most passionate advocate. You've got the love and the long-term perspective that justifies all the effort for slim financial rewards. You've got every motivation to succeed in the booking business, including perhaps the fervent desire to get to where you don't have to do it anymore—where you've built enough of an audience and buzz that it's financially worthwhile for an agent to represent you.

Booking yourself also gives you a lot of control, contacts, and knowledge, said Rani Arbo, who booked her bands Salamander Crossing and Daisy Mayhem for years.

A lot of the coffeehouses book very much on personal taste and not on hype, because everyone is in it for the love of music and the committees are very invested in having their own personal say in who comes. It's not like a performing arts center where they kind of have to book on hype or on reputation because they are going for a bigger audience. They don't have the time, they don't have the volunteers, and they don't have the same sort of investment to go through mountains and mountains of stuff in press kits.

So I think the smaller circuit is totally bookable by an individual. It is a lot of work, but on the other hand, it means that when you show up you've actually had conversations with the promoters, you've established a relationship, and if you know the right questions to ask and how to put the contract together, you have an incredible amount of information as to what is going to happen when you get there. For me, dealing with four people and travel and everything, that was actually a source of some comfort.

—RANI ARBO

At the grassroots and local levels, booking is a relatively straightforward (though not easy) process, and it isn't a disadvantage to be booking your-self—some venues actually prefer dealing directly with artists. The lessons that I've learned from performers, agents, club bookers, and my own time in the booking trenches can be boiled down to a few simple precepts.

POLISH YOUR PRESS KIT.   Your press kit tells venue bookers, clearly and concisely, who you are, what you've done, and what your music is like. You may need to present or mail a physical press kit sometimes, but most booking people (and media people too) will head to your website, where everything should be easy to find. Here are the main elements you need.

PHOTOS.   Sure, we all want to be judged by what we sound like, not what we look like, but good, professional photos are essential. Make sure *you* are the focal point and not the background, so your mug will still be seen if a photo is reproduced at thumbnail size. You should also make high-resolution photo files available on your website, so that a booker/promoter can download them for posters and other publicity.

SONGS.   You need a sampler of your best songs. Tracks from your most recent release are the obvious choice, as long as they're representative of what you do in your live show and the first couple of songs make your musical point (I know it's unfair, but judgments are often made on the basis of brief samplings of one or two tracks). If you've got strong studio tracks but they are quite different from what you do onstage—if, for instance, you recorded with a band but you perform solo—you should supplement them with a few concert recordings or demos that represent your live sound.

LIVE VIDEOS. For booking, good performance videos are arguably even more important than good audio tracks. What better way to convince a booking person that you can deliver the goods than showing a video of yourself doing just that in front of a happy crowd? The more closely the venue in the video matches the venue you're trying to book, the better. If you're seeking house concert gigs, get footage of yourself killing it at a house concert, and ditto for a band show at a club. Not only will videos help you get gigs, but the venues will use them for promoting the show.

BIO. The bio is your chance to characterize your background and music in the way that you want to, and often your exact words are reproduced in entertainment listings or venue calendars. Make it as brief as possible—attention spans are extremely short in this overloaded era and getting shorter all the time. I recommend having three versions of your bio available:

- Twenty-five words or less, for calendar listings and other tight spaces;
- 100 words or less, when you've got a bit more room to introduce yourself;
- Up to 250 words, for your website bio.

As with all good writing, be specific—evoke sounds and styles that people know. Don't boast that the music is unclassifiable or you don't sound like anyone else, even if you think that is the case. That is extremely unhelpful to booking folks who need to get a quick handle on what you do. If they book you, they will need good descriptive hooks to draw an audience to hear you.

QUOTES. Supplementing the bio are quotes about your music compiled from wherever you can get them—press, deejays, bloggers, venue owners, other artists. As with the bio, shorter is better; a three- or four-word phrase that really captures the spirit of your music is golden. If you're starting out, you may have to do a lot of soliciting to get any usable quotes. Obviously a well-known source gives the quote more impact, but a few words from even an obscure website adds authority and shows you've been out in the world playing.

CONTACT INFO AND LINKS. Along with the bio and quotes, list the pertinent contacts for booking, management, and publicity (which could all be just yours truly), plus links to your website and social media profiles.

ONE SHEET. A one sheet boils down your press materials onto, you guessed it, one page: photo, bio, discography, contact info, and links. You can print the one sheet to send with a hard-copy press kit, and also make it available online. Editing everything down so that it fits comfortably on one page (without using microscopic fonts either!) is a great exercise. In addition to your artist one sheet, you should make a separate one sheet for each new album that includes release date, label, and other details, and highlights any key tracks.

STAGE PLOT. This isn't part of a press kit, but it's something that a booker/promoter may request after you get booked. The stage plot is a one-page illustration that shows how/where you and your band members normally set up, and it lists your tech needs (number of inputs, DIs, microphones, mic stands, AC power outlets, and so on). Make life simpler for everyone and have this available on your website.

DO YOUR HOMEWORK ON VENUES. To find venues, look online at itineraries of artists at your level or slightly above and compile a list of possible venues—and be realistic about where you would fit in stylistically and how big a draw you actually have. Take note of ticket prices too. It's much better to do well at a small venue than to aim too high and wind up with a painfully slow night at a bigger place than you are ready for. Get venue recommendations from other musicians. When you book a gig somewhere away from your home turf, ask the people at that venue to recommend places that you might play on the way in or out. When you contact those other venues, be sure to mention where you're already booked—that automatically gives you legitimacy.

Be creative about venues, too, and keep your eyes open for all the sorts of alternatives we discussed earlier in this chapter—house concerts, openers, music stores, and so on. You may need to do some lower profile appearances at first in order to be seriously considered for a full headline slot. No matter how much they like your record, venue bookers may want to see you play before they schedule you for your own night.

FIND THE BOOKING GUIDELINES. Venue bookers have preferences about what they are looking for, of course, and how they prefer to be contacted, and all this may be spelled out online. Check it out before sending anything. And if no guidelines are posted, call the venue and ask whom you should contact. If you can't connect with the actual booking person, someone else at the venue can probably give you this information and tell you when/how to follow up. (If you send an email but it goes unanswered, as often happens, try the phone during business hours.) Get the name of the person you speak to, and when you're following up, mention that you spoke to so-and-so. Referencing that contact raises the odds of your music getting a look and a listen.

FOLLOW UP. Until you get to be famous, you have to do more than call or email, submit your music, and wait for the phone to ring with offers for high-paying and glamorous gigs. You have to call again a couple weeks later. And call again. And call again. And call again. And call again . . . You may feel like they're being rude or you're being a pest, but you are just doing what you have to do, because there are many other musicians and agents trying to get the attention of the same individual. No response doesn't necessarily mean that your music has been carefully checked out and deemed inappropriate for the venue; it means that your inquiry got lost in the piles, or (best case scenario) that your music *did* get checked out and placed on a list of possibilities, where it will forever remain unless you follow up. Gigs go to those who persist.

When you're going through this process, you have to steel yourself against being ignored and rejected over and over again, and keep at it. It's really hard and it really sucks, but try not to take it personally; it's more a reflection of the crowded world around you than it is a judgment of your music. If you're feeling very discouraged, talk to another musician struggling with the same thing—it'll make you feel less alone, at least. (You also might check out a little book called *Rotten Reviews and Rejections*, which compiles scathing commentaries on books subsequently deemed to be classics.)

> *You should not expect to be treated with basic courtesy by venue bookers. They will usually not return phone calls or emails or listen to and evaluate your music on its merits. But if you persist, you will find gigs, however modest, and if you do well at those gigs, you'll find your audience. You may find bigger and less jaded audiences off the beaten path. Build your audience one at a time, and those real human connections will sustain you.*
>
> —Andrew Calhoun

Band together.   As you try to make headway in the world of booking, it's very easy to fall prey to feelings of intense competition and jealousy toward your fellow musicians. It's true that there are many, many of you out there trying to do basically the same thing, but musicians have so much to gain by cooperating with each other. Other singer-songwriters are people with whom you can share bills, contacts, tips, and travel expenses; they understand your crazy quest and are your best support group and source of comic relief.

You can band together professionally to do things that would be very difficult or impossible to do on your own. Many singer-songwriters successfully co-headline shows (your audience plus her audience equals enough bodies to fill a bigger room), do group tours (organized by label, region, stylistic affinity, or just friendship), and collectively put on showcases at industry events that are prohibitively expensive to do alone. Sometimes they wind up creating a formal organization. Affiliations and collectives of all sorts have become common in the indie music world, and for good reason: there's power in numbers.

Get organized.   The more gigs you do, the more you need to develop a system for organizing all the information associated with booking them: contact information for the various people at the venue (booker, manager, sound engineer), directions, sound check and performance time, equipment needs, capacity, financial deal, ticket price, anything else supplied (food and drink, groupies, green M&Ms), places to stay, local press and radio contacts for publicity . . . It's a good idea to keep a checklist of these items so you can email it or fill it out as you're talking on the phone. That way, you and the venue booker are clear on the details, and you know what to ask for and what to expect when you show up. (A side benefit is that you've probably impressed the venue with your professionalism.) A lot of these details might be formalized in a contract, too; the venue may have a standard contract, or you can create a performer-friendly contract by adapting one from another musician/agent or using a published sample.

Paper files or a notebook will work fine for a small amount of booking information, but the more you perform the more time you'll save by going electronic. Eventually, you may want to build the kind of database that an agent (or marketer) would use, or buy a program specifically designed for that purpose.

BUILD ON YOUR SUCCESS.   If you want to gain momentum as a performer and step up to the next level, keep in mind that a scattershot approach to gigging will take you only so far. The same principle discussed above for opening slots—that you should always have a follow-up plan—applies to all the gigs you do. Rather than randomly chasing down whatever gig possibilities pop up, wherever they may be, you can follow a general game plan in which one show builds on the last and the one before. Here's one such scenario, described by Brandon Kessler, who founded the indie label Messenger Records.

> When you're starting out, try to build a regional following around your hometown. Start by booking shows at home, then build outward in concentric circles. It's important to revisit the cities where you have played, as you want to keep the momentum going. Make sure to promote your shows. Call the promoter at the club and ask for a local media list for press and radio. Send them CDs and a bio with the tour date listed, and follow up with them.
>
> If you work hard to promote the shows (that is, hand out flyers, contact the press and radio, and get posters and flyers displayed around town and at the local record stores), the promoters will notice. They will be encouraged

to give you better shows on better nights of the week with bands that draw more people. If you work diligently, and people like your music and are willing to pay to see you, you can build a regional following. Then you can network with artists in other regions and offer to trade shows with them (they can open for you and vice versa). And then, of course, you want to revisit the cities where you've played.

I can't stress enough the importance of selling CDs at the show, keeping a mailing list at the show, and letting people know your Web address by handing out flyers. The mailing list is absolutely crucial, as your following is everything.

—Brandon Kessler

The real world is always unpredictable, for good and bad, and performers need to be ready to jump on unexpected opportunities as well as recover from unexpected calamities. But a thought-out plan helps focus your efforts on gigs that pave the way for better gigs down the road.

AGENTS AND HELPERS

Let's say you've gotten yourself off the ground as a performer. You've played a widening circle of clubs and have a record out, some press clips, and a growing fan base, and now the opportunity presents itself to get some help with the booking. Before you kick up your heels and happily turn over booking responsibilities, it's important to understand the workings of this relationship from both sides.

Perhaps there is someone else who loves your music nearly as much as you do, a friend or fan or patron saint who volunteers to pitch in. Should you take up the offer of this kind soul, who's got great intentions but knows nothing about the music business? Here are a couple of perspectives on that question, first from singer-songwriter Andrew Calhoun, who founded the artists' cooperative label Waterbug Records, then from booking agent Jim Fleming, who has represented artists from the coffeehouse level on up through a star attraction like Ani DiFranco.

What I saw with Waterbug was that every single time that artists got help with booking (with the exception of major players), they ended up with big holes in their schedules because the agent dropped the ball. There isn't enough money at this level to attract and motivate quality professionals. You need to bite the bullet and do all your own booking and promotion, until such time as there is such demand for you that you haven't got time to do it. Which may never happen. It's a lousy office/ sales job just like any other, but it will allow you to practice your art. When people offer help, let them gather contacts, then follow up yourself, because chances are, they won't.

—Andrew Calhoun

If you can find a person whose is as passionate about your music as you are, has some business skills, and is smart and willing to learn, that could be somebody very valuable for you to form a relationship with. I believe that as in any relationship, the key thing is to be patient. You stay in touch with each other frequently and acknowledge what the hurdles are and what problems you are having, and acknowledge your short-comings too.

The thing that I have heard consistently over the years from artists is that it's really hard for them to get on the phone and sell themselves, and that's why they want someone else selling for them. But the fact is, if they've gotten to the point where someone is interested in representing them, they have *sold themselves and know much more about that than the person who's going to take it over. Use that information to teach. In a way I think it's valuable to do it yourself for a long time, because then you are able to tell if that person is doing a good job or not.*

—Jim Fleming

Booking is, as Andrew Calhoun noted, a sales job, and if you're going to be represented by someone who does this for a living, you need to consider the hard numbers. For many performers, there just isn't all that much money involved. Booking agents work on a percentage basis: 15 percent, or maybe 20 for a less-established artist. The artist typically supplies everything that goes into the press kit—CDs, photos, printed material—while the agent covers postage and other expenses. With this arrangement, lining up low-paying shows can be a case of what booking agent Nancy Fly called "rabbit starvation."

> *Rabbit starvation is where it takes more energy to hunt, kill, dress, and cook the rabbit than you gain in nutrition when you eat it. So a lot of gigs that we book for a brand-new artist, if the artist is making $100 or $150, we're losing money, because it costs more than our 15 percent to book the date. But that's still something that we are willing to do if we feel that the artist is going to develop and will be able to make $2,000 to $2,500 pretty soon, and then we'll be in the black again. So that's why I say when you are a developing artist, you have to get somebody who's absolutely in love with what you do, or you've got to do it yourself.*
>
> —NANCY FLY

Of course, the agent isn't the only one affected by rabbit starvation. If you are making $100 a show, does it really makes sense to hand fifteen or twenty dollars over to an agent? More to the point, is this agent accomplishing something that you couldn't do yourself? Just as agents are sometimes willing to work for a meager fee in the short term because they see potential in the longer term, the rabbit-starvation scenario makes sense for you only if you believe the agent will eventually land better-paying, higher visibility gigs than you could line up yourself. It's worth keeping in mind that an agent with low overhead (working solo or part-time from a home office) can afford to invest more time and effort in developing your career than can someone at a larger agency, with rent and payroll and all the other office expenses to meet each month.

This is a business relationship between you and an agent, and you need to treat it as such. But, as I've said, when you are establishing yourself as a performer, you want to work with someone who sees more than dollar signs in the future. An agent or publicist with a passion for your music will do a much better job selling you, and will be much more patient and persistent at the early stages. The higher you rise on the music business ladder, the less important this passion becomes—at some point, the money is enough to justify the agent's effort. With big stars, booking becomes a matter of negotiating rather than selling; the music has already proved itself and found its audience.

If a professional agent sees enough potential in your career to justify working for a while at the rabbit-starvation level, he or she understandably wants some kind of guarantee that you won't skip off to another agent as soon as you're established. That's why an agent agreement might include a term: say, three years, after which the agreement might be renewed or terminated. Before signing an agreement like this, be sure you understand exactly what is expected of you and what is expected of the agent. And in *any* long-term agreement, advised lawyer Wayne Rooks (whose firm has represented such independent spirits as Ani DiFranco, Moby, and Pete Seeger), build in as many "out clauses" as possible, so you don't get stuck if specific benchmarks are not met.

A good agent brings contacts and experience in the booking business beyond what you have, and opens doors that you as an independent artist could bang on all day without having anybody answer. But don't expect an agent to—*poof!*—perform miracles. Just as performing is only one facet of being a singer-songwriter, the booking agent is one cog in a bigger wheel.

It doesn't really make sense to get a booking agent until you are trying to promote a CD nationally. And a booking agent is part of a whole team: you need to have national publicity and a national booking agent at the same time. A booking agent is not going to do much with you if your re-cord's not getting any airplay and if you don't have anybody calling the radio station and setting up on-air interviews for you and things like that, because nobody will come to your gig. You might be able to get a gig once, but nobody will ever ask you back.

—NANCY FLY

And none of these things—the gigs, the publicity, the airplay—happens without the great songs and the gift for connecting with an audience. Take care of the business, but don't let it sidetrack you from what's truly essential: getting better and better at your art. Even (or especially) in this marketing-saturated age, there is no more powerful advertising than word of mouth, carried by those who leave a show with that special glow from a night of great music.

IN THE STUDIO

When I first got the songwriting bug and the attendant desire to capture my creations on tape (dateline 1977), the four-track cassette recorder seemed like a godsend. It was such a leap beyond the boombox with the tinny built-in mic, allowing fledgling songwriters such as my brother and me to try out some of the rhythm and harmony parts that were beyond the capability of two voices and four hands. With a borrowed bass and drum machine (featuring ultra-cheesy handclaps that were completely irresistible), it was possible to simulate on a crude and sometimes comical level the backup band we fantasized about having.

But as cool as all this was, the hissy sounds of the multitrack cassette could not be confused with the glossy productions coming from my favorite LPs. That was the realm of the professionals—of pop stars and masterful studio cats laying down tracks with mixing consoles as big as my bedroom. With few exceptions, home recording was for personal expression; the major labels held the keys to the world of commercial recording, opening the studio doors only to those with holy-grail record deals and big budgets.

The reality for musicians today is startlingly different. Plenty of high-profile pop music still comes from those slick players, fancy studios, and major labels, but professional-quality recordings can come from anywhere else too. With the arrival of the DAT machine in the '80s, high-quality live digital recording became possible in any living room or at any gig; with the ADAT, multitrack digital recording came within the reach of home studio mavens with a bit more money and ambition. Those twin inventions let the genie out of the bottle, and nowadays a laptop and a microphone is

159

practically all you need to make an album. You can record on your own time, at your own pace, and for an array of purposes beyond making a full-length album: to work on new songs, to experiment with arrangements, to make a demo, to collaborate, to release a single, to record sound for a video, or simply to share songs with friends and family.

These changes in recording technology have fed right into the growth of independent and artist-owned labels from a fringe phenomenon to a significant and far-reaching channel for new music. A big part of that story, too, is the evolution of the Internet and its powerful tools for interacting and doing business directly with music fans. So along with the major labels and their marketing muscle, there are many other tiers in the record business today, from large independents on down through individual artists selling self-produced, self-released CDs off the stage and from self-designed websites. In other words, this is a world of many options and opportunities beyond waiting for a megacorporation to come along and turn your songs into gold records and Grammys. A new kind of power— and responsibility—is in your hands.

> When I first started, you hoped and prayed and worked and hopefully you'd get a record deal. There was no such thing as making your own record or doing any of the things that you can do now to start a career and work it on your own. There's been a radical change. The technology and access to dissemination, either through the Internet or any other ways, have made it so much more of a do-it-yourself thing, with people building viable careers when on the surface no one has ever heard of them. To me it's remarkable.
>
> —CHRIS SMITHER

> You can actually sell or give or share your music with the whole world. You don't have to have the middleman. Availability has always been the trick gate that record companies have stood in front of. For most musicians, it's like, "You can only get through this gate through me." So then it means, "You have to jump through this hoop first, and then I'll let you go in." You don't really have to go through that anymore. You can make your own website and get your music out there. It comes down to this: if the music is good and it has something to say and it has something to offer a

listener, then that listener has the wonderful ability to make that choice. He wants it, he gets it.

I can tell you for a fact that in the 1960s, for every hit song or every hit group that made an album, I probably would much rather have the demo they gave the company than the album the company made. It's still the same. Make your own music. Get the atmosphere around that song that you want. And the people will hear it and will feel it.

—RICHIE HAVENS

Even as the tools and the business of recording have changed in fundamental ways, the creative challenge remains the same. How do you take these living, breathing songs of yours and convey their essence in a fixed medium? Should you dress them up with other instruments or present them as you wrote them? Where is the magic balance between sounding polished and professional and nitpicking all the life out of your tracks? How do you communicate with fellow human beings when you're sitting alone with headphones on staring at a microphone grille? And how do you make the technology serve the music rather than the other way around?

More than ever, the artist is the one answering these questions, rather than a producer or manager or A&R department. There is no one-size-fits-all scenario for recording—each artist and each project is unique. But there are key issues, some philosophical and others purely practical, that every recording musician needs to address. Some of the most important decisions are made long before you press the record button, so let's start back in the planning stages.

GETTING READY TO RECORD

There is something seductive about having your own album. I'll never forget the moment I finished burning the first copy of a home-recorded collection of my songs and popped it into the CD player. Those amber numbers ticking off the seconds on my tracks gave me an instant feeling that after more than twenty years of playing and writing songs, I was finally a *real musician*.

Friends and fans, too, reinforce the feeling that having a tangible, saleable product of your own is the sign of being serious about your art. They will urge you to make your first record and your next and your next, and you want to satisfy them—and yourself. So the desire and the motivation to record are often very powerful, and the technology that makes it happen is within reach.

In the flush of excitement about amazing gear and shiny discs, however, one essential question is often glossed over: not "What should I record?" or "How should I record?" but "Why am I recording?" As noted above, there are many potential purposes for a recording project. Know before you start why you are doing it, and keep that intention in your sights. The process of capturing sounds, turning knobs and sliding sliders, and hearing a song take shape is so absorbing that it is easy to forget why you're doing it—and you emerge weeks or months later, bleary-eyed and broke, with something that doesn't really do what you set out to do, and with important projects (like new songs) left unfinished.

The first thing to realize is that the world already contains a staggering amount of recorded music, much of it piling up on shelves or sitting in dusty boxes. I personally have been on the receiving end of review copies of new records for many years—more music than I could ever hope to check out fully while still eating, sleeping, and making a living. Music critics like to pretend that they hear everything and know exactly which records and artists are the best, but if they were honest they would admit that great music escapes their attention every day while they rave about other music that they may barely remember by next month. I've heard more than a few people in the music business joke about the need for a law requiring musicians to wait a certain number of years before making a record, like waiting to buy a handgun. It can be depressing to think about this, but it's a truth that must be acknowledged.

The flip side is that none of the other stuff out there is *your* music, and there's always room for another voice and another creation. At some point, you need to block out everything else and throw yourself into making the music that only you can make. But if you want to make a record for sale to the general public, be sure that it meets two criteria: you are ready, and the material is ready. Consider these thoughts from two people in the record business: Jim Olsen, co-founder of the singer-songwriter–oriented indie label Signature Sounds, and producer Dawn Atkinson, formerly with Windham Hill and Imaginary Road Records.

Don't rush your art. I really feel like many songwriters are in such a rush and fall in love with the recording process so that before they know it they have four or five records that have sold minimally. The industry doesn't care, and the audience is a little confused because they don't know which record to buy.

I think an artist needs to be out there testing the material live. Just because you have ten songs doesn't mean it's time to make a record. Maybe you press up a bare-bones record with just you and guitar so you have something to sell at gigs and give to club owners and such. But hold off on that debut album until you feel like this is a piece of work that really represents the best that you can do. And when you do cut that album, realize that until people hear it, it's a new record. It can be a new record for two or three years. Make sure you work it from every angle so you get as many people to hear it as possible before you create a glut of product that doesn't really have an audience yet.

—JIM OLSEN

Don't make a record until all the songs are great. There are certain artists that I can remember working with whose first record was fabulous, the second record was pretty good, the third record was worse, and they start making too many too often. They become better at their craft of writing songs but not necessarily better at the quality of the songs. They've had a whole lifetime to collect material for their first record, and then they have a year and a half, or however long it is, to do the next one. Maybe they have some rejects from the first album, but they all of a sudden have a time frame that they have to write in. That's a big problem, because what if you don't come up with great songs in that time frame? What do you do—postpone your album release, or just put something out because you want to keep the momentum of your career going? A record company would say, put something out. I think that's wrong. I think you are better off working on it longer.

*I think that's the hardest thing—keeping up the great songs. And then
also, don't be afraid to sing someone else's great song.*

—Dawn Atkinson

As Jim Olsen suggested, it is possible to meet the demand for a recording
to sell at gigs and use for promotion while still waiting for the right moment
to unveil your "official" debut. In fact, making a recording or two without
the pressure of making *the* recording is a very good idea. Especially if you are
used to live performance, the studio might seem like an alien environment
for making music. You're sitting in front of highly sensitive microphones,
your ears encased in thick headphones, conscious of the need to deliver
something special while trying not to worry about the time (and money)
ticking away. Without an audience, you have to generate your own energy
and communicate with people you can't see, who may not hear what you
are playing until years later. Here's how two accomplished performers
described the conceptual leap that you have to make to get your best
music on record.

*It's a very different mental process. You have to really concentrate on where
you're sending your energy. It's not as obvious, so it takes more focus. You
have to imagine that you're sending your music not at the microphone,
but into the microphone and into the wire and into the machinery and
into the tape and into the speakers and into the person and into the heart.*

—David Wilcox

I remember back when I used to do the Prairie Home *show, I was always
fascinated with the fact that Garrison [Keillor] seemed to have such a
sense of the radio audience, and I never really did. I was just playing to
those people there in the World Theater or wherever we were, and he had
this remarkable sense of people out there in their yards or in their living
room or on a boat, listening to the show. I might have learned something
from him about that, about being able to imagine when you're making a
record that you are playing for people.*

—Greg Brown

Studio playing also requires very close attention to sonic detail. In this
laboratory-like environment, mistakes that nobody would notice during a

live show can be distracting and bothersome. Some of your best tricks onstage might not hold up under the scrutiny of a recorded take that will be heard again and again and again; by the same token, there are nuances you can exploit in the studio that would be completely lost in performance. When you're recording, you have to play and sing more cleanly than usual, yet you need to be loose enough that your take has soul and guts. It takes time to adjust to all this, explained the veteran session player, producer, performer, and recording artist Jerry Douglas.

> *The studio is a different place to play music than the stage. You're not getting feedback from the audience. Every note you play is under a microscope, but the cool thing about it is, you get more chances if you need them. It goes both ways: I know a lot of recording musicians who say, "Oh, I can't play in a band in a live situation—I am just not good at it." And with a lot of road musicians, you get them in the studio and you start hearing things that you didn't hear live—maybe some rough edges, a lot of noise, things that you just can't do in the studio.*
>
> *It depends on what kind of music you are playing, I guess, but if you are trying to be smooth and you're trying to fit into a track, you want to really listen to other people and try to play as cleanly as possible. Try to put the best thing on tape that you can with a low noise ratio. And that's really hard for a lot of people who come in and don't know how to sit in front of a microphone, who've never played in a band situation sitting down or with headphones on. If you want a consistent sound on your instrument or on your vocal, you can't be jumping around like you've got an SM58 in your hand onstage.*
>
> —Jerry Douglas

You don't want to be learning these lessons while paying for studio time. It's very discouraging, not to mention expensive, to deliver a spot-on performance and then discover that it was ruined by your squeaking chair or explosive "p"-pop in your vocal mic. So set yourself up at home to make demos: work on your microphone technique, sing while wearing headphones (if it feels really strange, try using the headphones on only one ear), and if you're planning to overdub parts, practice with a multitrack setup. Listen critically to the results, and correct any problems you find.

Demos also present the opportunity to assess the state of the material, make some final edits, and experiment with arrangements. How well do the songs translate? What other sounds might be needed to bring them alive? Are any lyrics not quite there yet? Is the song structure tight, or are there places where you need to add or subtract?

In songwriting workshops I tell people, [imagine] if a painter said, "Well, now I'm going to go paint my masterpiece without any sketches and without any little plans." It took me a long time to figure out that if you get the recording equipment—just a little simple setup—and tape the stuff and listen back to it, or goof around with arrangements before you go into the studio, it's really helpful.

—PATTY LARKIN

While these demos can help you work through questions and streamline the process that will follow, don't fuss too much over them, overdubbing endless tracks and trying to perfect every last note. Think of a demo as a sketchpad rather than your final canvas, a place to clarify and capture your ideas. A sketch that is too carefully rendered begins to compete with the artwork it's supposed to support.

Demos are dangerous, because you create a good demo, and then you're trying to re-create it when you get into the studio or when you get onstage, and that's difficult. I don't like doing that. You can't finish a song on a demo. You should just throw down the idea and "That's it, we'll get to it later," because those lame drum beats can really take all the fun out of a good song.

—ALANA DAVIS

When you've made a satisfying demo, with the basic arrangement and feel you're looking for, that recording can be a very useful reference in the studio. In particular, when you're getting ready to record an album track, I recommend checking the tempo of the demo to see if you are close. With the excitement and time pressure of the studio, it's very easy and common to play too fast and not to realize it at the time—I learned this the hard way on an album project where we had to redo several songs that we'd rushed. Referencing the demos, or just keeping a list of target tempos by beats per minute, would have headed off this problem and saved significant time and money.

As you plot out a full-length recording project, make sure you take a step back to consider how well the material as a whole hangs together. It's tempting to try to pack everything that you can do onto a record—particularly your first—but you might wind up with what producer Malcolm Burn called the "Kellogg's variety pack" ("Here's our fast song and here's our slow song and here's our country song and here's our reggae song"). There's something so powerful about a record with a point of view. It's like a house with a distinctive look and style when viewed from the street; inside, each song is a room that has its own purpose and decor but relates back to the overall architecture. Your opening song invites people in the front door, then track by track, you lead them on a walking tour of the interior. Listeners can really lose themselves in a record like that.

Considering your recording project in this light also forces you to think about who those listeners are—or who you hope they will be. Can you picture a particular person or group of people grooving to the album you're going to make? Are you creating a keepsake for fans of your solo show, building a band sound for rock-oriented listeners, trying to cultivate a new audience? Imagining your listeners will help inspire soulful performances and guide you through what can be a byzantine process.

Perhaps the ultimate example of the targeted audience approach is the songwriting demo, made expressly for pitching a song to another artist to record. In music business centers like Nashville and L.A., an entire industry is built up around making demos for professional and wannabe songwriters. While songwriting demos these days typically feature full-band instrumentation to give producers a taste of what the final record might sound like, they are an entirely different animal from records made for commercial release. The goal is not to highlight the unique personality of the songwriter, but to present a recording artist with a perfect vessel into which to pour his or her own personality—it's like pitching a screenplay to a movie star with a tailor-made (and sexy and heroic and touching and flattering) starring role. This gives a certain slant not only to how a song is recorded but to which song is selected in the first place, pointed out Kyle Staggs, who, while working at Bug Music, pitched songs by many singer-songwriters for covers by other artists as well as for use in film, TV, and other media.

> *Singer-songwriters generally write very personal songs. It's a cathartic thing for them—they're writing about their lives, about their friends' lives. So sometimes these songs are not really coverable by someone else because somebody else hasn't had the same life experiences. Or the song is not usable in a film because even though the sentiment is perfect, the words don't fit the scene that's going on. Music supervisors are very conscious of the words in a song.*
>
> *That having been said, I think that most singer-songwriters have a song here or a song there that doesn't really fit in those parameters. They write a song that's a little less personal or that's so personal but applicable to a whole wide range of people, or it has a big instrumental section in the middle or something like that; and all of a sudden a music supervisor is interested in it or someone could cover that song.*
>
> —Kyle Staggs

When it comes to making a demo of a song that fits these requirements, marketing considerations influence the sound and feel of the track. The demo might feature a singer hired for a general (but not *too* close) similarity to whomever the song is going to be pitched. Sometimes there are multiple demos—one with a male singer and one with a female singer, or perhaps one with a full band and one with piano and vocal, each made to appeal to particular producers or artists. Songwriters like Beth Nielsen Chapman who double as singer-songwriters (and there are not many musicians who successfully straddle these two worlds) are highly conscious of the difference between recording a song for themselves and for someone else.

> *When I go to make a demo of a song, I'm not going to necessarily make my record of it. I'm going to put it in a mold that is less defined by my voice, and I wouldn't put like a tuba on it or a conch shell. . . .*
>
> *I don't really tell people they should go get a whole [fully produced] demo, because sometimes the song is not good enough. Especially an aspiring writer might still be in development; they go and spend thousands of dollars, and as they say in Nashville, "You can't polish a turd."*
>
> —Beth Nielsen Chapman

HOME vs. STUDIO RECORDING

As noted above, one of the biggest benefits of the digital revolution is that high-quality recordings can be made anywhere—in studios of all sizes, on stages of all sizes, in the living room or kitchen and basement, in a church, in a cabin in the woods . . . Many recordings are made in different environments at different points in the process: the songs are recorded at home, then edited, mixed, and mastered in the studio; basic tracks are recorded at home, then sent to other musicians who add tracks in their own home studios; band tracks are recorded in the studio, overdubs happen at home and other locations, and then all the pieces are put together back in the studio. The point is, you can customize the process however you want—the technology is ready to travel.

What you're looking for is a recording site that makes you feel comfortable and creative, that inspires you to play your best and has the technical capability to capture that moment. For some, recording in the wee hours at home might summon the most powerful tracks; for others, a pro studio is a better choice. So what's the best environment for you and your project? Here are some important trade-offs to consider.

YOUR OWN TIME VS. BORROWED TIME.   When you book studio time, unless you are in the enviable position of having many hours and dollars at your disposal in which to fiddle and daydream and wait for inspiration to strike, you have to rise to the occasion when the red recording light goes on. You are on a schedule, and you have to be focused and efficient. Even if you woke up on the wrong side of the bed and don't feel much like playing music that day, you have to get yourself in the mood: it's stand and deliver.

On the other hand, a studio comes with an engineer, so you are relieved of the burden of running cables and twiddling knobs, and you can concentrate on playing the music. I remember home-recording sessions with my band when it took so many hours to get set up in the evening (after our respective day jobs) that by the time we were ready to record it was two in the morning, we were exhausted, and the beginning of the next workday was looming. The gear was finally ready to capture good takes, but we were no longer able to deliver them. By contrast, a skilled engineer in a pro studio will quickly dial in the sounds so your energy doesn't wither while you chase down mysterious buzzes and do test take after test take.

Perhaps the biggest advantage of a home studio is that you can record songs whenever you feel like it. And if you try one night and everything sounds really lifeless, you can just do it again another night—and the knowledge that you *can* redo things will probably loosen you up and encourage you to take more chances whenever you play. That's what the Milk Carton Kids found when they recorded the bulk of an album in empty theaters while on tour, rather than working in a concentrated block of studio time.

> *We never succumbed to the what can be stifling pressure of thinking that this next one has to be the one. To be able to engineer this sense of plausible deniability for yourself, where every time you're doing a performance you think that's not going to be the one, I really enjoyed that.*
>
> —JOEY RYAN

If you're recording at home, ideally you have a dedicated space and can leave the gear set up, or your gear is simple enough that you can set up and lay down a song before the inspiration fades.

> *When you have your own place, it's like your laboratory. You can experiment with it. No matter how much you rent a studio, very few people will really go in there and spend two days experimenting. When I built this [home studio], we spent a day trying to find the right place in the room to put the bass. . . . And since most of what I do is the same kind of instruments, now I have places worked out.*
>
> —DAVID GRISMAN

Speaking of time: when you are budgeting time for a recording project, no matter where you are going to record, I suggest that you make your best guess about how long it's going to take, and then double it. That'll give you a closer estimate of the time actually needed. Recording sucks you into a twilight zone where hours and days disappear without a trace.

JOEY RYAN, THE MILK CARTON KIDS

BUYING VS. RENTING GEAR.   In a rented studio, other people are responsible for buying the recording gear and learning how to use it. When something breaks, they need to fix it. When something better comes along, they have to decide whether it's worth the investment. That's a huge responsibility to take on, and it can quickly lead to gear obsession and what producer Gurf Morlix (Lucinda Williams, Slaid Cleaves, Robert Earl Keen) calls the "money-pit studio syndrome." Leaving gear matters in somebody else's hands allows you, once again, to focus on writing and playing the music, which is more than enough to keep you busy.

But if you always rent or borrow gear for recording, you do not, as the Marxists say, own the means of production. You are not entirely in control of the recording process, and you're not really learning its inner workings. Now, is that a good thing or a bad thing? It depends on your gear personality—are you a gearhead, gear challenged, or somewhere in between? One strategy that makes sense for a lot of musicians is assembling a basic recording rig at home for songwriting demos, practice recordings, straightforward solo tracks, and overdubs, but heading for the studio for more complicated ensemble work.

It's damn near impossible to cram a band into your bedroom and record them and have it actually sound good, unless you've got professional engineering capabilities.

—JOHN KEANE

Another possibility is to supplement a home recording setup with rented or borrowed equipment (better microphones and preamps and so on) when it comes time to do a full-length project. Or, as noted above, you can do parts of the project at home and parts in the studio—these days it's very easy to transport tracks back and forth.

If you do decide to put together a home studio, be prepared for the sinking feeling you will get when the piece of gear you bought last year—when the pro-audio gurus agreed that it was the best deal out there—is suddenly considered to be, well, last year's model. Recording technology changes as fast as computer technology—which makes sense considering that much of it *is* computer technology. Look for equipment that has proven its value and quality over a period of years, not months, and that can be upgraded rather than tossed out when the time comes. And remember that there's a lot to be said for really knowing a particular piece of gear (and a particular room) inside and out, so you can just plug and play rather than begin the learning curve all over again with something new.

Among engineers and producers I've spoken with, there's a pretty clear consensus that for acoustic recording at home, high-quality microphones and mic preamps are your best investment in recording gear (that is, after your instrument—great sound starts at the source). Mics and mic preamps never become obsolete, and they have a much more significant impact on the sound than does your recording platform. The first time I recorded at home with good microphones, I was amazed at how straightforward the whole process became. I just pointed the mics in the general direction of whatever noise I was making, and they sounded sweet—the baseline quality was high enough that further experimentation was purely optional. And with really nice sounds going down the mic cables at the beginning of the signal chain, many of the fancy effects and mixing functions I had at my disposal became unnecessary. As the saying goes: garbage in, garbage out. The corollary is true too: good stuff in, good stuff out.

SIMPLICITY VS. VERSATILITY.   From my perspective, you should record with the simplest setup that allows you to do what you need to do. Endless options can so easily lead to endless futzing: filling all those tracks just because you can, trying this and that and the other effect even though the first one sounded pretty damn good, and so on. It's fun to experiment with new ideas, but too much of that can sidetrack you from serving the song. Technical limitations can be good for creativity, because they force you to rely more on the auditory receptors attached to the sides of your head.

> *You can make a record on a ghetto blaster if you need to. You can make a record for any amount of money, and it can still be good. You don't have to have state-of-the-art gear. Basically I think you have to have ears. My studio is somewhat limited. It's in a house. I don't have a bunch of great gear. I've got a few nice preamps and a couple of nice microphones. But I feel like the limitations of that really help me keep things simple.*
>
> —GURF MORLIX

If your project is focused entirely or primarily on your solo sound, your recording setup can be dead simple and located just about anywhere. If you're using microphones, the room has to be quiet enough that the sounds you want to capture aren't drowned out by traffic and neighborhood noise. It's when you start introducing other instruments and people—particularly drums—that a full-fledged studio becomes much easier to work in. Issues of soundproofing and isolation of instruments have already been addressed there, and if you want to do something similar at home you'll have to spend a lot of time propping up mattresses and devising other sound-deadening baffles. The more instruments you're dealing with, the happier you'll be to have the additional channels, microphones, and other gear available in a studio.

ISOLATION VS. TOGETHERNESS.   Engineers generally like having clean separation of sounds, with each instrument on its own track(s) and bleeding onto the other tracks as little as possible. This way, they can easily edit and process each track without interfering with the others. In terms of the recording environment, this means that they will want to build the song track by track or to isolate you and the other musicians with walls, windows, and baffles. If you're accustomed to jamming in a circle in the living room, it can be disorienting to have your bandmates disappear from view and be audible only in your headphones, or to barely glimpse them over baffles, panels, and foam. The way you set up to record is always a compromise: sometimes you have to sacrifice a little sonic isolation to create a better ensemble feel, and vice versa.

Any approach to ensemble recording can work. But the point is, in choosing *where* to record you should think about *how* you'll to be able to play in that space—a function of layout and location as well as the capabilities of the equipment.

ENGINEERING AND PRODUCING

The recording environment is more than the room and the gear—it's defined by whoever is working with you. Today's technology encourages musicians to be self-sufficient, taking the tools and the process into their own hands. But as the songwriter and performer, you are already wearing a couple of big hats. Is it possible or advisable to also take on the roles of engineer and/or producer? That's an important question, and it begs another: What do those people actually *do* in the studio anyway?

The job of the engineer is more straightforward and consistent from studio to studio and project to project. The engineer is in charge of setting up the gear and dialing in the sounds; it's a technical job but a musical one too, because the shape and impact of the notes you play and sing are at stake. Producers are involved with all this stuff too, but the real nuts and bolts are in the hands of the engineer. If there's no producer, the engineer works directly with the artist in making his or her ideas happen. This can be an appealing arrangement for experienced musicians who know what they want to achieve in the studio and how to communicate their preferences. Years ago I paid several visits to the storied home studio of mandolinist David Grisman in northern California, where he worked with a young engineer who knew the gear and the space inside out. When an impromptu session arose—as it frequently did when Jerry Garcia or another of Grisman's pals stopped by—the engineer needed only a short time to get ready to roll tape, so the musicians were free to just *play*. The recordings that came out of that room clearly reflected the atmosphere of casual creativity.

Compared to the engineer, the producer is a more mysterious figure. Producers are often attributed with tremendous powers: they're credited as the alchemists behind chart-topping albums and blamed for commercial and creative disasters, as if the artists themselves were only tangentially involved. Joni Mitchell once said the producer "laminates you to the popular sounds of your time" and that producing her own records allowed her to remain true to her compositional instincts. Yet producers themselves sometimes describe their role in much humbler terms; in the words of T Bone Burnett, "A lot of what a producer does is make tea."

Broadly speaking, the producer's job is to get the best possible album out of an artist. That involves particular sets of skills and tactics for each artist and each project, but there are some commonalities in what producers do.

HELP SELECT AND SHAPE THE MATERIAL. We've already talked about the editing and filtering of songs you need to do to get ready to record. A producer facilitates that process and brings a fresh perspective that can be particularly valuable for a singer-songwriter. Here's how Jerry Douglas described the back and forth between producer and artist in the preproduction phase.

*Normally what you're doing is going through a bunch of songs, and some-
thing might strike me that they didn't hear or the other way around. If
they don't write a lot, you might want to get them fired up to write more
or get them excited about their writing and improving their writing.*

*When I used to do Tim O'Brien's records, he would come out with this
big armload of songs and he'd say, "These are all terrible." He lived with the
songs, and he didn't really get outside of himself with the songs sometimes.
They were incredibly deep songs, and we just shaped them and gave them
arrangements that made them hold together and instrumental parts that
helped even more to tell the story. And then they started to look like
something. He would be happy—he would laugh out loud, "I didn't know
this was in the song!"*

—JERRY DOUGLAS

Beyond helping to improve individual songs, a producer might also
have a clear idea of the whole album and how to give it a distinct identity.
As the artist, you are on the long road of writing, playing, recording, and
developing, and it's harder for you to see this one project as separate from
everything else you do. A producer zeroes right in on the impression that
this particular recording will make.

*If I'm falling in love with the songs, I can usually get a pretty good idea of
what the record will sound like right away.*

—GURF MORLIX

TAKE CARE OF BUSINESS.   Along with doing the conceptual and creative work,
the producer deals with such unsexy things as budgets, deadlines, and
label input. On a simple project with a small label, these administrative
matters might not add up to much, but every little detail you have to take
care of is a potential distraction from making the music.

HIRE THE SUPPORTING CAST.   Unless he or she doubles as an engineer, the
producer brings in the engineer(s), who may or may not come attached to
a studio. Many producers have engineers they work with regularly and rely
on for particular types of sounds, which is good because you're getting a
team with a (literal) track record.

Unless you have a regular band or are going solo, the producer also assembles whatever session players are needed to bring to life the record you're collectively imagining. Even if you do have a band, sometimes a producer needs to gently suggest that the drummer sit out a particular song, or that bringing in a pedal steel player would be cooler than having the guitar solo that usually happens. Better that someone else make that sort of comment and judgment than you.

DIRECT THE RECORDING PROCESS.   A producer may rely on an engineer to oversee the technical details of the recording process, but he or she will at least lay out the basics of where and how the record is going to be made. That includes the critical question of how you and the other musicians will be set up (playing together in the same room, playing together but separated, building the song track by track, or some combination of the above).

CHEERLEAD.   Great records begin with great performances, and a producer does whatever it takes to make them happen. That means getting everyone jazzed about the material and then setting the right vibe in the studio, so all the players feel relaxed and confident. It means being diplomatic and encouraging, and knowing when to actively direct and when to just get out of the way. As T Bone Burnett suggested, it might mean making tea at the appropriate moment. (Patrick Simmons of the Doobie Brothers told me that the producers of the band's early albums believed that alcohol fueled their best tracks, so he was duly supplied with Southern Comfort along with his guitar when recording solo pieces. That's an anecdote, not a recommendation.)

A good producer is your ally in the studio, someone who recognizes your strengths and knows how to work with and—ultimately—help you stretch beyond what you thought you could do. When the producer/artist chemistry is right, it transforms the process of record making and even songwriting. Chris Whitley once described how during a dark period when "I didn't have the confidence to even know whether I could stand what I was writing," renowned producer Craig Street (Cassandra Wilson, k. d. lang) helped him believe in his songs again and keep the new material flowing. Even though the record they made at the time (*Dirt Floor*) wasn't "produced" at all—it was recorded in one day in a barn, live and solo—Street had played a central role in making it possible.

So, given this general job description for a producer, should you produce your own record? Malcolm Burn's advice is crystal clear.

> *Don't. There's a reason why producers have their jobs, and it's not because they are money-sucking leeches. It's because they bring something to a project that can only be gained by experience and knowledge and good taste and maybe a great record collection. You still need some people around who have that experience—to know when a good idea is a good idea, to know when a bad idea is just not worth pursuing, to know what a great sound really sounds like and how to get it.*
>
> *I think if you can afford a producer, you should have one. Self-production is probably not a great idea, especially if you're in a band and want the band to be around awhile. You need somebody there to field the questions, to be the middleman, to do all the things that nobody else wants to do.*
>
> —MALCOLM BURN

Not everyone agrees with that assessment of self-production: some musicians love having complete control over the process, and they feel that a producer is an unnecessary intermediary who dilutes their ideas. But even for these determined do-it-yourselfers, there are essential helpers behind the scenes—at the very least, an engineer, band member, session player, manager, or friend who can act as a sounding board. If you really try to go it alone as singer/songwriter/player/engineer/producer, you risk getting lost in a house of mirrors, where you're overwhelmed by all the reflections and don't know which is your true face anymore.

> *It's really hard to sit there in your home studio and make a record and be sure that it sounds like you want it to sound. You need another person to bounce things off of. Everyone who produces their own records has got one. They've got somebody else around and they can go, "Listen to this. Give me your honest opinion. Have I gone over the top with this?" Or "Am I loud enough?" A lot of people who produce their own records will not mix themselves loud enough.*
>
> —JERRY DOUGLAS

If you're seeking engineering or production help for a recording project, be sure to ask candidates for other work they've done. If none of their sample recordings sounds remotely like what you want to do, keep looking. You want proof, not promises, of what they can deliver. The whole process will be much smoother and quicker if they normally work with music and production values similar to your project and you can agree on specific recordings as a reference point.

Pay attention, too, to your gut feeling about what it would be like to hole up with a particular person for hours or days and share the intimate process of creating music. Will you feel comfortable, respected, free to speak your mind, ready to take chances? Or might the situation turn out to be awkward and tense? For good or bad, the mood that pervades the studio will be memorialized in your recorded songs.

MAKING TRACKS

The recording studio these days is a perfectionist's paradise. A song can be assembled piece by piece on virtually unlimited tracks, and then each individual sound can be edited at a microscopic level of detail. Real-time performances become waveforms on a screen that can be cut, pasted, altered, combined, and repaired ad infinitum. Wizardly powers are at your fingertips, and it's easy to get so consumed by the creative and technological possibilities that you never complete a project.

There is something to be said for having a limited amount of time. It forces you to get it over with. I've seen people get a Pro Tools rig at home and start recording songs and never finish them. They end up keeping everything they do and have to sift through it all later on, and they just get totally lost.
—JOHN KEANE

As intoxicating as the process of using these tools can be, what you have to remember is that in the end the process doesn't matter. Listeners respond to your final mix, and they won't know or care how you got there;

what they care about is how the words and music make them feel. In the studio, you have to take off your wizard's hat and put yourself in the position of those listeners, hearing the song for the first time. At every turn in the recording process you need to ask yourself, "Am I enhancing their experience or just doing cool studio stuff because I can?" And, by extension, "Am I giving my own song the treatment it deserves?"

In recording, as in all musical pursuits, what works for one individual would be ineffective or inadvisable for another. Through experimentation and experience, artists learn how to coax the best music out of themselves in the studio, and how to translate those moments into a stream of data that will come alive for someone hearing it through car speakers or the home stereo or ear buds at the gym. It's an ongoing quest—at the end of every recording session, it seems, comes a scheme for how to do things a little differently next time. Here are some tips and tactics to use in your ventures behind the studio glass.

Watch the interplay of your instrument and voice.   As a singer-songwriter, you have developed a subtle and sophisticated partnership between your vocal and instrumental styles. When you're singing, you adapt your playing to better support your voice and stay out of its way; and when you are playing, you sing differently than you would if your hands had no job to do but hold the microphone or make photogenic gestures. These adaptations are largely unconscious—you don't really notice how much the two functions influence each other until you try to separate them in the studio, as engineers often like to do so there's no bleed between vocal and instrument mics.

> *When I separate the voice from the guitar, to come back and do a voice track, I begin to intellectualize and think, "How should I sing this?" When I play guitar I'm not analyzing.*
>
> —Patty Larkin

When I did separate vocal and instrument tracks for the first time, I found that my backup parts suffered the most. The groove was weaker, and my playing tended to be too busy—I wasn't giving the vocals enough breathing room. Like Patty Larkin, I got self-conscious in a way that I never do when the vocal is demanding my full attention. But with practice, I got better at playing without singing, and I grew to appreciate the advantages of this approach—both for the vocal performances and for flexibility at the mixing stage. On my most recent album I wound up doing it both ways: I played and sang together on about half the songs, the ones for which getting a live feel was particularly important, and I overdubbed vocals on the rest.

The same considerations apply to a session in which you are singing over other people's backup: pay attention to what happens when you sing separately from your core accompaniment.

> *My first record was live, but it was solo. And the second record, the band recorded while I was in the control room, and then I would do separate days of vocals where I would listen to the band on my headphones. And it didn't work for me. It made me sing careful and cautious—not to mention there's no audience, I am in a quiet room, and it's really loud in my ears. It was just different.*
>
> —JEWEL

BE SPONTANEOUS.   If everything on your record is thoroughly planned out, labored over, and polished to a high gloss, it will sound that way. Music gets a charge of energy from accidents and ideas that emerge (or combust) in the moment; that's what makes it sound like humans having fun playing songs rather than a computer spooling out rows of code. So crack open the studio door to serendipity; as Beck once said, the moment when the pizza delivery guy interrupts your session could be the best part of the track.

Taylor Goldsmith of Dawes described how *The New Basement Tapes*, for which he (along with Elvis Costello, Jim James, Marcus Mumford, and Rhiannon Giddens) wrote and recorded songs based on rediscovered Bob Dylan lyrics, was a lesson in letting go of perfectionism in the studio.

> *It reminded me of how fun recording and music can and should be. We really learned how to let go and not worry too much about how good something is going to be or how to cultivate our own comfort zones. I feel like the result ended up being so great because of that. It's very easy to get precious about records that you make, and the music is often better served not to do that.*
>
> —TAYLOR GOLDSMITH

If you are building a song instrument by instrument, you can still inject spontaneity into the proceedings—in fact, when you're doing a lot of overdubs it's especially important to loosen up so the music has that elusive live feel.

You have to pay attention to it the whole time so you don't lose it. Part of it is being spontaneous when you're overdubbing: overdubbing inside the control room where the mic is picking up what's coming off the speakers, things that enhance a live feel to the tracks that you're putting down on top of everything. And then not getting so precious on every little thing really helps.

—AMY RAY

It sounds paradoxical, but there are ways in which you can plan to be spontaneous in the studio. Chris Thile once told me about a clever tactic that producer Alison Krauss used while he was overdubbing vocal harmonies on a Nickel Creek album. On the band's mischievous cover of Carrie Newcomer's "I Should've Known Better," Krauss had Thile improvise harmony part after harmony part while listening to the lead vocal. She never played back the parts he had already recorded—she just asked for another and another and another, bang bang bang. When they finally did audition all those parts together, there were strange and evocative cluster harmonies, with the various lines moving around, across, and sometimes against each other—the kind of thing that could only come about by accident, and a brilliant match for the off-kilter feel of that track.

LEAVE THE BARK ON IT. That's Jerry Douglas' phrase for not fussing all the life out of the music. There's a difference between a mistake that jumps out and draws attention, and a little blip of not-quite-perfect playing or phrasing that nobody else but you is ever going to notice. It's much easier to distinguish between a fatal flaw and a harmless lapse in somebody else's performance than it is in your own, so gather some additional opinions before you decide how to proceed.

In considering whether to fix a mistake, you have to weigh what will be gained (one place in the song that you can now listen to without grimacing) versus what might be lost (the organic feel of that section). Remember that the bark is what makes a tree look like a tree—and keeps it healthy and alive. Cut off the dead limbs if you like, but leave the bark.

LISTEN TO THE LOGIC. When you perform a song from beginning to end, there is a natural logic to the way your take unfolds. Phrase B sounds like it does because of the way you played Phrase A; Phrase C builds on an idea you happened upon in Phrase B, and then Phrase D brings it to a conclusion. A slightly garbled word on one chorus leads you to emphatically declare it on the next repetition. Stretching for that high note on the bridge makes your voice a tad hoarse early in the next verse. All these little connections are what make that rendition of the song a unified performance.

With the powerful editing tools available today, you have to pay close attention to this chain of action and reaction. Unless you want a jarring crosscut effect, avoid cutting and pasting things together that just do not follow each other because they are divorced from the context in which they made perfect sense. The same problem can arise when you go back to change something in a track that you recorded at another time: when you first did the track maybe you were completely wired from that double espresso and cinnamon roll, and today you're feeling much mellower and so will have a hard time matching the mood and feel of the original.

If you are unhappy with a few sections of a track that you generally like, sometimes it makes more sense to do the entire thing again so you get a second performance that's cohesive and has that internal logic.

For me the stage is an immediate, visceral, highly exposed, vulnerable place, and making a record is kind of vicarious. . . . The fact that there's no audience in the studio is a hurdle for me to begin with. I just can't sit around and try to make the perfect vocal and the perfect guitar track. I lose artistic inspiration for that kind of obsessiveness. So what I've learned to do is to record a bunch of different times, because the song as you play it on any given day is just that day's interpretation. I thought, "OK, if I can't sit for a week and think about a song in the studio and play it a hundred times, then maybe I could record a bunch of songs this week, record all those same songs four months later, somewhere else, and then do it again three months later." Then you have a few different versions that happen in the moment,

but you can put them against each other and say, "OK, this one sounds
most like the song, and that one, I don't know what we were on that day."

—Ani DiFranco

Use that first-take feel. There's something special about the first take or
two, when the song feels the freshest. Don't squander that moment by
playing the song all the way through multiple times while warming up or
testing levels. Save your first real, full-throttle performance for when the
gear is ready, because subsequent takes may not have the same spark.

As Ani DiFranco suggested, you can capture multiple first takes if you
allow for rest time in between. That can be a good alternative to bludgeoning
a song over and over until you can barely stand to play the opening chords.

Try it live. If a live ensemble feel is what you are seeking, the sometimes
overlooked or overruled way to achieve it is to play that way. Never mind
the crowded room with all the wires and stands to trip over, or the difficulty of fixing mistakes because everyone is bleeding onto everyone else's
track. The gain in energy and synchronicity might more than offset the
loss in technical control. Just as there's a logic to a solo performance, in a
band performance there's a dynamic give and take between the musicians
that doesn't happen in the same way when the parts are overdubbed.

What a difference to listen to a track and then just go into a room by
yourself and play along with the track, versus going into a room with four
awesome people and having eye contact and playing off of each other. It's
entirely different. Granted, record making and live playing are different
crafts, but it doesn't seem to me as though they can't cross here and there.

—Alana Davis

Rodney Crowell described how later in his career he found himself going
back to '50s-style recording—sitting in a circle without headphones.

To record without headphones makes it entirely about performance.
What's your primary goal: production or performance? I'm only inter-
ested anymore, really, in performance as it leads to production. You know,
using the tools of modern recording to lay down everything in the most

polished, clean, and tidied-up way doesn't interest me. I'm interested in the collaborative performance. When we're all gathered around and the drummer has to lean over to hear what I'm playing on the acoustic guitar and what I'm singing, he can't play just banging on it and listening to the singularity of what he's doing. You have to come together.

—RODNEY CROWELL

RODNEY CROWELL

GET IN A BAND STATE OF MIND.   Of course, recording the band live isn't always possible or even preferable. When you are overdubbing individual parts, don't forget that you still *are* a member of the band. Those are people playing in your headphones, not just static tracks. Close your eyes and lose yourself in the flow of sound.

> *Being your own band . . . sure, it's hard. But why not grow, why not learn how to do it with feeling and make it sound like it's live? Because if it's living in you at that time then it* is *live, even though it's not happening at the same time. What is the difference between me sitting in here and another guy in there, playing on two different tracks, and me playing one part and then going in there? If you can really lock in on the tape, it's your mind that makes it live.*
>
> —MICHAEL HEDGES

CONSIDER THE CLICK.   One way that studios facilitate the piece-by-piece recording of a song is through the use of a click track—the metronome ticking in everyone's headphones that keeps them on time and puts the tracks on a precise tempo grid. I've made records both with and without a click, and there are clear tradeoffs that are important to consider.

The biggest advantage of the click is that it helps you get the band in sync and diagnose rhythm problems, and it makes editing a breeze. Plus, if you have multiple takes at exactly the same tempo, you can easily copy bits of one take into another.

The disadvantage of the click is that humans don't naturally play music with machine accuracy. We get excited and speed up, we slow down as the ending approaches, we extend a pause a little just because it feels good. The primal pulse of music is more like the heartbeat than the metronome.

In my view, the decision of whether to use a click or not should be made song by song. In some songs it is extremely helpful, even essential, while in others it's stultifying.

GET SOME DISTANCE.   In recording as in songwriting, you often need a little mental and physical distance to judge the results. Songs will sound very different at another time and another place and on a different set of audio equipment. So after you have listened to your freshly made tracks in the studio, come back the next day and see if they strike you the same way. Take the tracks home and hear how they sound on your stereo. Listen in your car. Play them at a low volume and listen from the next room, or while you are doing the dishes, and take note of which elements you can hear. Are the most important things (such as your voice) coming through? Try the same exercise with one of your favorite albums—is the balance very different from the balance on your songs?

Although it would be nice if everyone listened to our recordings through gleaming audiophile sound systems in acoustically optimized rooms that are otherwise silent, the world just isn't like that. That's why pop producers who work in big-budget studios take tracks out to their cars and play them through cheap speakers or ear buds as a final test. If the music sounds good there, it'll stand up anywhere.

GET A SECOND OPINION.   As discussed in the section on producers and engineers, it's essential for those working on their own to use another person as a sounding board. You start off with a clear idea of what you're trying to achieve, but deep into the process you might find yourself wondering if you're heading in the right direction or if your original idea was totally misguided. The quickest way to break out of this maze of uncertainty and self-doubt is to get a second opinion from someone whose taste and honesty you trust. Even if you don't take their advice, an opposing view can help clarify where you stand.

SUBTRACT AS WELL AS ADD.   With all those empty tracks laid out in front of you, it is always tempting to add sounds. And add. And add some more. Go ahead—pull out the didgeridoo for the intro or sing your tenth harmony part. But be sure to listen back to see if you've really added something or are just filling space. It's a good exercise to put all the faders down to zero, then bring the tracks in slowly, one by one, starting with the most important ones—the vocal and main rhythm parts. You might be surprised to discover that what seemed essential doesn't really contribute that much to the mix.

I'm not one of these people that will throw all the colors of paint at the canvas and then scrape it off. I absolutely choose the colors I like and then put them on. And so if something doesn't need anything, then I don't put anything else on it.

—KT TUNSTALL

You don't have to make records that are complete structures. You can let people guess at what the other stuff might be, use their imagination for what might be there. It's great sometimes when you think you hear something in a piece of recorded music, but it's just your brain filling in what you want to be there at a particular point of time. To me, that's always a good point to stop.

—CRAIG STREET

BE A SONGWRITER, THEN A RECORDING ARTIST. The most important preparation you can do for a recording project isn't shopping for new equipment, reading recording magazines, or even making demos; it's working on your songs. When you've really put heart and soul into the writing and come up with your best material, the recording process is so much simpler. You're not trying to use studio tricks to manufacture excitement and intrigue in a track; you're spotlighting the excitement and intrigue that's already built into the writing. Your job in the studio becomes so much clearer, and the gear so much less important.

People are now so consumed by technology, and there's so much of it available, but the only thing that really differentiates one person from another is who's got the best ideas and the most interesting musical concepts. I'm not interested in who's got the coolest microphone and the best mixing board or whatever it is they've got. At the end of the day, there's no substitute for great ideas.

—MALCOLM BURN

THE LABEL CONNECTION

Let's step out of the studio now and consider how your spanking new recording might make its way into listeners' hands. What are the pros and cons of going the do-it-yourself route? What do traditional labels have to offer? How about a small independent label versus a larger indie versus a major?

The most compelling reason to be your own record label is control. You decide what sort of record to make and when to release it. You decide how it's packaged, how it's publicized, and how you want to sell it or give it away. Unlike most artists in the history of the record business, you own the master recordings that you make and the songs that you write, rather than having signed them over to a company that has its own agenda and short-term interests. You are in charge of your own destiny—both creative and financial.

> *Record companies are always looking to jump on a trend and give it a modern sound, but the things that make it sound modern now will make it sound dated in a few years. My back catalogue is quite valuable to me, and albums I did five years ago still sell quite well. I spend most of my life building a new audience, and my entire catalogue is new to my new audience. Because I'm in a field where I'm not doing trend-oriented stuff—in fact I've consciously steered away from that—an album of me just playing solo guitar is going to sound the same in thirty years as it does now.*
>
> —HARVEY REID

> *If you create it, you're not going to wait around for some big company to sign you to a label. You don't wait around for these people to acknowledge you. Meanwhile, sure, you make less, you learn to live cheap, you really learn to find your wants and needs in a sensible fashion. But, at a sub-industrial level, you make all the artistic decisions—not the people in the front office, not the people who try to shape your image—and that's what keeps the material flowing and fresh. When you give in to their system, when you become a bought person and they're going to give you wealth, power, and fame, and the creative decisions are then being made more and more by the people in the front office, all you can begin to write about is your personal sense of alienation.*
>
> —UTAH PHILLIPS

The downside of being in charge is that, well, you are in charge. You have to hire and pay the large cast of characters involved in making a record: the studio, the players, the recording and mastering engineers, the photographer, the graphic designer, the duplicator . . . All these expenses add up fast, so you either need to make a substantial investment yourself or ask others to back you—and you may have to scale down your ambitions considerably (a string section would be really cool on that one song, but maybe next time). And along with paying for everything, you have to *do* everything yourself or oversee the work of others who are helping you. If you are acting as your own publisher, you have to copyright the songs and affiliate yourself with a performing rights society (see "Music Publishing Basics"); if your album includes covers of other people's copyrighted songs, you have to get mechanical licenses and then track and pay royalties; and you need to copyright your recording itself. And then you have to figure out distribution, publicity, and the rest . . . Handling all these administrative matters is a big job, which is why many artists find a partner for running their labels—a manager is a natural choice.

> *I think a lot of people have this impression that I'm a colossal control freak, that I have to do everything myself. But once you make the decision that you're not going to work for a corporation and you still want to make music, there's nobody else around to do all of that stuff, and for years I've coveted the help of, for instance, a graphic designer. It's only recently that I've had the money to pay people or the phone number to call when I need help of a certain sort.*
>
> —ANI DiFRANCO

When you put out an album yourself, you also become the sales force behind it. You're not relying on singles, advertising, and retail promotion to stoke up the demand for your music. Your primary sales tool is getting your butt up in front of people and playing your songs so well that they just have to buy your album after the show (and then tell their friends to buy it, too). Thanks to the Web, you can have global distribution, but in reality the odds of selling your album to a random Internet surfer are mighty slim and getting slimmer all the time just because of the bazillions of other albums out there; the Web functions mostly as a very handy place where people who have heard you or heard about you can track you down and see, hear, and read more. You sell fewer copies with this person-to-person approach than you might with mass marketing, but because your operation is so lean and you have no middleman, you keep a much higher percentage of the money that does come in.

> *I remember years ago when I was working with Warners, our agreement was that I could buy my stuff at cost and sell it on the road, those kind of places. Well, their cost was twice as much as what I actually had to pay to manufacture it myself. I said, "How is that?" And they said, "Well, we have big buildings filled with secretaries and limousines and lunches and stuff like that." I didn't have any of that, so the cost of me doing it . . . it didn't make sense to go with a large label, especially nowadays with the Internet and people can buy and trade and listen to stuff whenever they want worldwide.*
>
> —ARLO GUTHRIE

One rung up the record-business ladder are small independent labels, run on shoestring budgets by people who love the music (if they didn't, they—like you—would find a more sensible way to make a living). When you sign with a small indie label, you may get help with the promotional and administrative matters mentioned above, plus maybe financial support for making the record; in return, you are sharing a portion of the revenues. A good label has relationships with press, radio, and retail that are very hard or impossible to develop when you're putting out release number 001—or even 006—on your own label. The imprint of an established label gives your album credibility in the business as well as with consumers. If the label is doing its job (and that's always a big *if*), your album's odds of getting into people's hands, getting reviews, and getting noticed at all are higher than if you were handling these areas yourself.

> *The main advantage of working with a label is in marketing and visibility. We obviously have more resources and invest more in publicity, advertising, radio campaigns, and such—things that are hard to do as an independent artist, especially if you're starting from scratch. And also being part of a roster of other artists, I think, helps to establish who you are and what your music is about. It puts you in a subset of artists. We've tried to put together the sort of roster where if you like the music of one*

of our artists, you are more than likely to like the others. We are trying to get a level of consistency.

—JIM OLSEN

One possible advantage of working with a small label rather than a large indie or a major label is flexibility in your contract. Especially if you've built a track record and audience on your own, you stand a better chance of negotiating a deal in which you own your masters outright and license them to the record company, or the label owns the record but all rights revert to you if it's no longer available in retail channels or if the company goes under. Maybe you can hold on to your publishing—the ownership and control of your songs' copyrights—an extremely important deal point for a singer-songwriter (more on that below). The details of an agreement like this are significant down to the last *hereinafter* and percentage point, so don't take chances: get a good lawyer to vet any contract before you sign it (not just record deals but agreements with agents, managers, and others on your team), no matter how much you trust and like the people you're going to do business with.

You shouldn't expect a small label, with its limited staff and finances, to turn your record into a runaway hit. A well-run indie can build on what you have accomplished on your own and help you step up to the next level, but it can't create that coveted thing called buzz out of silence. Even tiny labels are looking for artists who have already made headway in the business—selling their own records and, especially, touring actively and widely.

I advise artists to think about it from a label's perspective: How can a label sell my CDs? You can't rely on big radio play, because that is locked up by the major labels, who participate in payola-like schemes. Articles in the press help but do not sell lots of records. Therefore, artists need to tour and play in front of real people and make a concerted effort on their own to build a following. We work extremely hard for our bands, but we expect them to be doing the same.

—BRANDON KESSLER

Bigger independent labels have more money, more staff, better distribution, and correspondingly bigger catalogues to administer. The line is sometimes blurry between the largest indies and the major labels—some indies are distributed through the majors, and major labels have also bought up prominent indies and let them operate more or less autonomously in order to take advantage of their counterculture image and ear-to-the-ground intelligence about new music. In recent years, indie labels have also signed quite a few well-known pop/rock artists who've fallen from grace at the majors, so indies are more than ever working the stylistic mainstream.

From the artist's standpoint, dealing with a large and high-profile company can be a plus or a minus. It's nice that there is a team of publicists rather than just one, but are they dealing with so many releases each month that they are just turning the crank? If a former chart topper is your label mate, does that enhance your visibility or just steal the label's attention away from your record?

Independent labels pride themselves on having interests beyond the bottom line, but they still have rent and salaries to pay each month. The most stable and successful companies tend to have a handful of artists who sell enough records to bankroll the rest. The same is true of major labels—superstars generate the lion's share of profits. The difference is that an indie might keep the lesser known acts on the roster out of a sense of responsibility to the music, while the major will drop them as fast as they can.

They decide pretty quick if you're not going to be one of the few acts that pays the bills for all the other ones. If after three weeks your record isn't headed for platinum, they kind of lose interest.

—DAN BERN

Where major labels excel is in working with the records that are headed for platinum. They know how to milk that moment for all it is worth. Mass marketing is their forte, and music with a "cult" following is an uneasy and temporary fit.

Music-business cynics (and they are a large tribe) like to depict the major labels as masterminding some kind of evil conspiracy to force-feed cheesy music to the world. The reality, I think, is far less colorful and James Bond–esque than that. As with all big businesses, it's about the numbers. Major labels are happy to give free creative rein to artists who consistently make blockbuster records. If Renaissance lute music was suddenly selling

Dan Bern

millions of records, the major labels would dispatch all their A&R people to early-music programs to sign the next big star. We'd have videos of lutenists with gyrating dancers and smoke machines. The soft-drink ads and movie tie-ins would quickly follow. As long as recordings of Francesco da Milano's fantasias kept selling in big numbers, the labels would keep churning them out—and eventually the stores and airwaves would be saturated with the work of glamorous looking, marginally talented lutenists.

As soon as the numbers started to fall, all those lute slingers would be back on their own, and the labels would start sniffing around for the next big thing.

If you're great and you're a genius and you've really got something, you'll probably hit it big at some point and then you'll fade into obscurity because that's what the music business does. It's all based on the premise that it's got to be today's thing, and of course you can't be today's thing tomorrow, so you'll be yesterday's thing. You'll be out the door no matter who you are. You could be the Marx Brothers, Buck Owens, Elvis Presley. Tomorrow they'll be selling something else, so you'll be in the cutout bin, no matter if you sold three records or if you sold 300 million records.

Then, if you survive for another seven, eight, ten, or twelve years, you'll be rediscovered, because people, having not been able to think of anything new during those years, will gravitate back to the shit that they grew up listening to, and they'll start copying that. And then maybe, if you had a big enough influence, they'll come around and find you because you're still great at that and you originated it. So they'll just rediscover you and put your name out there again. And if you live long enough you could do this three or four times.

—DAVID GRISMAN

On that curmudgeonly note, let's turn to the pertinent question: Where do you and your record fit into this industry picture?

When you're starting out, the clear (and, for most artists, the only) choice is to put out your music yourself. It's the best way to get your bearings in the studio and in the record business, and it gives you something to sell at gigs and online and to use for promotion. Releasing your own album gives you a quick sense of whether the do-it-yourself approach suits you or not, which will help you plot out your next career moves. Even if your ultimate goal is to sign with a label, DIY success will give you leverage and know-how when you do go shopping for a record deal.

When you've built enough of an audience and reputation that a label is interested in putting out your records, you still need to weigh what this company might be able to do for you versus what you can do for yourself. Will you get significant publicity support when the record comes out and while you're out on tour? Will the record be visible beyond your gigs and your website? Are there opportunities for shared bills and industry show-cases with other artists on the label? More and more, even artists who are signed to small labels are expected to fund their own albums and marketing.

> *Many of my friends are trying to get their finished CDs placed with labels and are hearing, "Well, if you want to come onboard, we suggest you hire publicist X." Which leads them to think, "Wait . . . aren't you the record label?"*
>
> —PETER MULVEY

> *If you make a record that is bare bones, that is the singer-songwriter and maybe a couple other instruments and is basically about the songs—it's not about the production—then you'll probably sell it at a limited number of places. You're probably not going to do much marketing of it, and it probably won't get to radio. If it's sort of a representation of your live thing, a keepsake or something like that, do it yourself absolutely. What's the point of turning that over to a record company?*
>
> *Much of it is about initial financing. It seems to me that if you can fund an album without really compromising your own craft in the process, and you can fund the marketing of it yourself, then you are better off doing it yourself, because then you are going to end up owning a master and you are in control of your destiny. But if you don't have that kind of funding, and there is a company that totally believes in you and thinks that they are really going to help build your career and make you a priority and do the right kind of marketing and sales positioning—and especially if they are going to help tour support—then you are better off being with a company.*
>
> —DAWN ATKINSON

It's tricky to compare the economics of an artist label versus an indie versus a major label, because they operate at completely different scales. You can make an inexpensive record, sell it on your own label in small numbers through limited channels, and promote it through low-budget solo touring—that can be a sustainable (though not necessarily lucrative) enterprise, because the expenses and revenues are in scale with each other. If you want to make a more complicated band record, you need to invest more up front and then sell more records to recoup the investment; more sales means, in turn, that you'll need to spend more on promotion; and if you want to take that awesome band on the road to showcase the record, you have to be playing bigger halls in order to pay and feed everyone, or else you have to subsidize the road work as a promotional expense (plus you'll need an agent who can get you booked in those halls in the first place). At that level of the business, the resources of a label become very attractive, if not essential. At a major label, the investment in production and marketing ratchets up so far (into hundreds of thousands of dollars to try to break a song on the radio) that only a serious hit is going to pay off.

> *If you sell five or six or even seven hundred thousand, that's kind of the low end of success for a major label. You are pretty much in danger of being dropped even if you sell that many, which for someone like me would be winning the lottery. So when you go into it independently, your whole plan is based on a completely different reality. You have to rewrite your success program and say, "Wait, what really is success and what's not? What will constitute enough? What will constitute satisfaction and a sense of having done really everything I could?"*
>
> —JONATHA BROOKE

The different scales of the industry explain why a gold-selling artist on a major label might be in debt and in danger of career crash-and-burn, while a troubadour who fills folk clubs with devoted CD-buying fans might be able to make a steady, although not cushy, living over the long term. In purely economic terms, you have to consider any potential record deal in light of the question: Which is bigger, a small slice of a big pie or a big slice of a small pie? The answer depends on the relative sizes of the slices and of the pies.

You're making a record that you hope will still be attractive and sale-able years from now, so you also need to think about what happens with the finances in the long run. And that's where ownership of the master recording and the songs themselves is so important.

> *I look at my copyrights as my retirement fund.*
>
> —HARVEY REID

Don't give your publishing away. Realize the value of your publishing. A lot of times what these labels are doing is throwing the publishing [into the contract], thinking that no one is going to question it because these younger or somewhat smaller artists are so happy to be getting a record deal that they don't want to rock the boat. They think that if they question the contract in terms of something major like publishing, they might scare the record label away.

The initial draft of a contract is usually the most onerous, and you should try to negotiate down from it. They expect to be negotiated with. You need to assess your bargaining position, of course. If they're doing you a favor and you go in and say, "Well, this change and this change and this change," they might come back and say, "Absolutely not. If you want this change, then that's a deal breaker." But at least by negotiating you've gotten to the point where you realize what they really want.

I would try to eliminate publishing entirely from the record deal. Sometimes you can't do that—sometimes the label is only interested in signing you if they can get you as an artist and as a songwriter. If you can't knock it out entirely, then try to limit it as much as possible. The best way to do that is after a set number of years the copyrights will revert to you, and if you do work out some sort of situation like that, be sure that the language in the agreement is very clear that it reverts on a certain date and that it reverts without further formalities, because you don't want to have to go to them and put them on notice and send a letter. You can get into a battle with the record label because they won't want to write a letter or they will take their sweet time doing it. So make sure that the reversion is clean and easy—that's a big thing.

—Kyle Staggs

No matter how you make your way through the tangle of the record business, remember that in the end everything comes back to you and your music. All a label can do is to brighten the spotlight on you and amplify the excitement that you're generating with audiences.

What's the work of a poet? To write poetry. What's the work of an artist? To paint. What's the work of a singer? To sing.

Fasten totally on the work. Give yourself completely to the work, till you can do it as well as it can be done, and then people come looking for you. But forget the rest of it. That will happen if you're completely fixed on the work. It's a superstition, I know; I believe it.

—UTAH PHILLIPS

TAKING CARE OF BUSINESS

If, like most working singer-songwriters these days, you serve as not only your own booking agent and record company honcho but your own manager, there are some more back-office business functions that will need your attention. Here are a few additional topics of particular importance to songwriters, including the basics of copyright and music publishing.

COPYRIGHTING YOUR SONGS

So you've got a spanking new original song—congratulations! Play it loud, enjoy the buzz of creation. But before you share your beautiful baby with the world, take a moment to make sure your work is protected by copyright, so you receive the credit, adulation, and compensation you deserve.

The good news is, if you have recorded or notated your finished song in a format from which someone else could reproduce it, then your song is *already* copyrighted. (In U.S. copyright-ese, your work is protected once it is "fixed" in a "tangible medium" that is "sufficiently permanent or stable to permit it to be perceived, reproduced, or otherwise communicated for a period of more than transitory duration.") No paperwork required: once your song is fixed, whether on a recording or a lead sheet with the music and lyrics written out, it's copyrighted.

CO-WRITING AND COPYRIGHT

When you're co-writing, it's important to pause at the moment when everyone agrees the song is finished and it's fixed in a tangible medium—in other words when the song is, by law, copyrighted—and document its ownership. Who contributed to the song, and what share does each person own? Is it an equal split, 50/50 for two writers, or one-third for each of three writers? Or are you the primary writer, so you own 70 percent while the friend who helped with a few smaller details owns 30 percent? You and your co-writers need to agree on a split and write it down—in an email or a piece of paper that everyone signs.

The reason to take this step, advised music publisher Randall Wixen, is to prepare for a common situation where later on someone adds material to the song—by rewriting some lyrics or the bridge, for instance—and asks for a percentage of the ownership. Documenting your original writer shares makes it extra clear that the song was finished and that this latecomer can't do anything to it, or claim any credit, without the agreement of all the writers. "You should lock it down as soon as possible to protect yourself so you can say, 'Here's when the clock stopped,'" Wixen said. "A lot of people will dilute your efforts without your permission even though they need it."

So why bother shelling out a fee to register your song with the U.S. Copyright Office? Basically, because registering the copyright bolsters your legal rights and provides evidence of your ownership in the public record, both of which could be important if there ever were a dispute over the song. In fact, you can't file an infringement suit in court unless the work in question has been registered. So there are good reasons to register a copyright, especially if you're publishing the song (that is, making it available to the public in some form). Registering a song close to its publication date gives you some legal advantages, but even if you wrote a song fifteen years ago and never registered a copyright, you can still do so now.

Copyright registration is a relatively simple process. Head to the Copyright Office website (copyright.gov), where you can submit or download the forms and get answers to many questions—the FAQ pages are very useful and actually written in comprehensible English.

For music, there are two basic types of copyrights with separate registration forms: PA, for performing arts, which covers the composition, and SR, which is for a sound recording. The distinction is critical: You can register a PA copyright for your original song, or for your original arrangement/adaptation of words and music in the public domain (a musical setting of a Shakespeare sonnet, new lyrics to the tune of "Old Joe Clark," "Oh! Susannah" arranged for ukulele and theremin). You cannot, alas, file PA copyrights for your ultra-cool arrangements of Beatles songs (that is, unless you get permission of the copyright owner . . . good luck with that). But if you make an album called *Tessa Troubadour Sings the Beatles*, you can register an SR copyright that covers the recording itself.

You register copyrights through the Copyright Office's eCO online system or by mail; doing it online is way cheaper. You can also save money by registering a group of songs as a collective work, as long as the authorship is the same for all of them. In that case, you give a title to the work ("Songs from the *Pain and Heartache* album" or whatever you choose) and then list the individual song titles so they are documented and searchable. It is possible, too, to register PA and SR copyrights together if the ownership is exactly the same for both; that would be the case if, for instance, you were releasing an album of all new songs that you wrote and are registering for the first time.

Using the eCO system, once you've submitted the application and paid the fee, you upload your files per the site's instructions. If you need to mail anything, you are given a shipping slip to use.

Once everything is received and found to be complete, the Copyright Office will send you a certificate of registration suitable for framing (or, at least, filing away in a safe place). That might take six months to a year, so what to do in the meantime? Play that song for people . . . and get started on your next opus.

TAPPING INTO THE PUBLIC DOMAIN

Let's say you've taken what you believe is an old folk song and written new words for it. Now you want to record the song that you created, and you sensibly want to make sure that you are free to do this without getting permission or a license. Songs that are in the public domain—often referred to as PD—are not under copyright, so you can use or adapt them however you want. But how can you tell if a song is in the public domain?

Ideally, you'd have your hands on original sheet music with a copyright date of 1922 or earlier—that's the best evidence a song is now in the public domain. But of course, the origins of many songs are tough to pin down, and you may find conflicting claims of who wrote or arranged a given song and when. If the song was published in 1923 or later, its copyright may or may not have expired, depending on whether the owner filed for renewal and on other factors.

The Web can help with your research. For an overview of copyright law and music, check out PD Info (pdinfo.com), which includes a list of songs presumed (but not guaranteed) to be PD as well as links to sheet music. Search the U.S. Copyright Office records (copyright.gov) to see if anyone's claiming a copyright. You can also look for composer and publisher information at the Harry Fox Agency's Songfile (songfile.com), ASCAP (ascap.com), BMI (bmi.com), or SESAC (sesac.com).

Stephen Fishman, an attorney and author of *The Public Domain: How to Find and Use Public Domain Writings, Music, Art, and More* (Nolo), pointed out that when someone copyrights an arrangement of a PD song, "All they own is what they add." And those additions are only copyrightable if they are more than "minimally creative"—they can't be "obvious" or "trivial." So if you want to use, say, a traditional blues for which various people have copyrighted arrangements, he suggested trying to strip away what has been added (the copyrightable portion) and work from the song's PD core. If there is such a thing, the original sheet music is the best source.

Many old songs, no doubt, fall into a vast gray area. Which means there's no simple answer except to do your homework, dig for the earliest version you can find (an interesting musicological quest, anyway), consult an expert if you need one, and know the ground you stand on.

PUBLIC DOMAIN RECORDINGS

It's important to understand that even if a song's composition is in the public domain, a recording of that song is probably not. At this point, copyright protection for the vast majority of sound recordings in the U.S. extends all the way to . . . wait for it . . . 2067. So, samplers beware: if you're working on a track and want to incorporate a sample from an old recording of, say, a gospel choir singing "Amazing Grace," you'll need to license it from the owner of the master recording.

MUSIC PUBLISHING BASICS

Once you've protected your songs by copyrighting them, the next important business matter to take care of is affiliating yourself with a performing rights organization (PRO). In the U.S., that means becoming a member of ASCAP, BMI, or SESAC.

What these organizations do is license music for public performance— at live music venues, on the radio, on TV, in bars and restaurants, in gyms, on airplanes, online, and so on—and collect royalties that they divvy up and distribute to their songwriter and publisher members. Which means that when your songs are performed at a club somewhere or played on the radio, you will theoretically receive a bit of money from your PRO. I say theoretically because the PROs can't monitor every performance of every song. They dole out licensing income according to a sampling of what is publicly performed, so the use of your song, especially outside of mainstream venues and channels, may not be monitored. (You can get at least some performance royalties headed your way, though, by giving your PRO the details about your own gigs—see "Getting Paid to Play Your Own Songs.")

Even if you're just starting out as a songwriter/performer and don't expect any royalties yet, you should affiliate with a PRO. That way you've established the channel through which money can flow to you whenever that happens, and also someone who wants to license your songs can find you: your song titles and contact information are in the PRO database.

It's worth noting that in the music community, the PROs have become controversial for their sometimes heavy-handed dealings with small venues; stories circulate regularly about coffeehouses and mom-and-pop restaurants that quit presenting music, or shut down entirely, because they say they

> **GETTING PAID TO PLAY YOUR OWN SONGS**
>
> You can actually earn royalties for performing your own songs at PRO-licensed venues, even small bars and coffeehouses, by providing that information yourself. ASCAP, BMI, and SESAC all have online systems where you can submit details about your gigs (venue, date, and so on) and the specific songs in your cleared repertoire that you played. That way you'll receive a portion of the licensing fees paid by these venues along with your regular royalty payments.

can't pay exorbitant PRO licensing fees (or defend themselves against legal action). It's beyond the scope of this book to address this hot and complex topic; suffice it to say that although it does seem that the PROs need to reconsider/reform their policies and rates for small venues, these organizations are still the only means by which songwriters can earn the income they deserve when their songs are performed. So if you want your songs to bring in performance royalties, you need to be part of the PRO system (and perhaps advocate for changing it).

Here are the basic steps to getting set up.

Go PRO.   Affiliating with a PRO is fairly straightforward process. You need to choose one society. For less established songwriters in the U.S. it's pretty much a choice between ASCAP and BMI, which are open to anyone; SESAC is selective. Ask fellow songwriters for their advice, talk to representatives from each PRO, and see who is the most helpful.

Once you've picked a PRO, go through its procedure to apply as a writer and publisher (assuming that you have not already assigned your songs to a publisher). You may need to pay application fees, but at this writing neither ASCAP nor BMI charges annual fees or dues. If you plan to sign up with a publishing administration service (more on that below), your administrator may be able to take care of affiliating you with ASCAP or BMI.

You don't have to apply as a publisher—you could just join as a song-writer and may, in fact, be told that's the way to go. But Randall Wixen, author of *The Plain and Simple Guide to Music Publishing*, recommended signing up as a writer and publisher because then you are aligned with the way the business works around the world: income is split between the writer's share and publisher's share, even if the writer and publisher are the same person.

If you are going to establish your own publishing company, you'll need to pick a company name that's not already used by someone else (and not too similar to an existing name either). It may take a few tries until you find a name that is approved. Once the name is set, you may need to file a DBA (doing business as) or fictitious business name statement and also publish a notice in your local paper—check with your county clerk's office to see what the requirements are in your state. Finally, you may need to open a bank account in your business name so you can actually deposit payments you receive.

CLEAR YOUR SONGS.   Once your application is accepted, it's time to clear your songs—which means submitting all the individual titles and their details to the PRO. If you've got a co-writer, you indicate how you are splitting the ownership as part of this process. (Your co-writer, by the way, needn't be a member of the same PRO.) This becomes routine maintenance: as you complete songs and release them to the world, make sure you clear the titles with your PRO.

GETTING HELP.   If you're starting out as a songwriter and acting as your own publisher, you may not need to do much beyond registering copyrights, affiliating with a PRO, and clearing your songs. But as your songs start traveling more widely, your job as a publisher becomes more complex. If a band wants to cover your song on their record, you'll need to issue a mechanical license. If someone wants to use your music in a TV show, film, commercial, or video, you'll need to become savvy about sync licensing. And so on. At this point you may wish you had a publishing administrator— that's someone who manages your catalogue in return for a percentage of the income it generates, while you retain ownership of your songs.

Until your songs bring in significant money through licensing of various kinds, it's probably not going to be worthwhile for a traditional music publisher to take on the work of administering your catalogue. These days there are Internet-based publishing administration services that are open to anyone (at this writing, options include CD Baby Pro, TuneCore, and Songtrust); they will register your songs internationally and collect royalties (mechanical as well as performance) in return for a sign-up fee and commission. You just need to assess if the additional income they might collect—beyond what ASCAP or BMI would already collect—is worth the cut that these services take.

Even if you decide to handle your own music publishing, you should seek out someone with knowledge and experience in this field—it might be a publisher, a manager, or a lawyer—who is available to help if/when the need arises. Having an expert you can call is particularly important these days, when opportunities develop at dizzying speed, said Wixen. A video might go viral and catch millions of views within a few days, and then suddenly someone is interested in using the song in a movie or a commercial. And that person will surely want an almost instantaneous answer—take it or leave it—so the pressure is on.

> *If someone calls you and says, "This song is perfect for our M&Ms summer campaign, and we want to license it—can we do it at five thousand dollars for a national commercial for a year?" you need to have someone in your pocket right away who can say, "No, it's worth seventy-five thousand dollars. Don't take the five grand they're offering you." You need to have at least some informed expertise at your fingertips so that you don't blow the opportunity but don't do something stupid.*
>
> —RANDALL WIXEN

PLAYING COVERS

In addition to managing the publishing for your own songs, at times you'll probably want to perform or record someone else's published song—like your crowd-pleasing cover of Stevie Wonder's "Superstition" (good choice!). Different types of licenses are required depending on the use. Here's a quick overview.

For a live show, the venue is on the hook for getting a public performance license that allows you to play "Superstition" and other covers. Usually venue owners buy blanket licenses from the PROs for use of any song in their catalogues.

If you want to release your own recording of "Superstition," in physical or digital form, you need to get a mechanical license—from either the publisher, an authorized representative such as Harry Fox Agency, or a song clearance service (see completesingersongwriter.com). As long as you follow the protocol, you can obtain a compulsory license for any published song and pay a set rate (at this writing, 9.1 cents per copy distributed for a song under five minutes).

If you want to post a video of yourself performing "Superstition," you'll also need to get a synchronization license from the publisher. There's no set rate, so you have to negotiate. (Yes, lots of people upload cover videos without getting sync licenses and get away with it, but they are taking a risk.)

Sampling a recording, by the way, is a different matter than performing the song yourself. If you want to use, for instance, a sample of that killer "Superstition" drum and clavinet groove in a song you're creating, you have to clear the sample with the owners of both the master recording and the composition. A sample licensing deal typically involves sharing ownership of the newly created song.

So be on the lookout for someone who can fulfill this role. When you get a licensing request and you're not sure if it's a good or bad deal, even a five-minute phone conversation with an expert may set you on the right track and make you feel much more comfortable and confident in a negotiation. And paying someone to spend a little time reviewing a contract could be a very worthwhile investment—both for getting you a better deal and for your peace of mind.

DIGITAL ROYALTIES

The CD market may have crumbled and traditional radio airplay may be locked up and out of reach of most musicians, but performances of music via webcasts, satellite radio, and other digital channels are a genuine bright spot in the recording business. Not only do these digital services play a much wider range of music than makes it onto traditional radio (known nowadays as terrestrial radio), but as a recording artist or even backup player you can actually get paid a royalty when your music gets played on Internet or satellite radio.

As discussed earlier in this chapter, there are two basic types of copyrights for music: one for the composition and one for the sound recording. When a song is released on record or publicly performed, the composition copyright generates royalties for the songwriter and publisher that are collected in the U.S. and distributed to members by the performing rights societies ASCAP, BMI, and SESAC. The sound recording copyright is often owned and licensed by the labels, and in this convoluted and highly contested area of music-industry law, terrestrial radio pays royalties for the songwriting/publishing but *not* for its use of sound recordings (though lots of people are working to change this). In the digital realm, though, webcasters et al. do pay both kinds of royalties, and in the case of sound recordings the rights are administered by a nonprofit organization called SoundExchange.

To make all this a little more concrete: when Janis Joplin's version of "Me and Bobby McGee" plays on an Internet radio station, a little chunk of change goes via the PRO to Kris Kristofferson and Fred Foster (as the songwriters) and to their publishers *plus*, via SoundExchange, to Joplin's estate and the owner of her record.

This digital performance right has only existed since 1995. "It's a new right," says Casey Rae of the Future of Music Coalition, "and if you were the songwriter and the performer and the sound copyright owner, you'd get the full revenue stream." More specifically, digital performance royalties are split like this: 50 percent to the owner of the sound recording, 45 percent to the featured performer, and 5 percent to backup musicians.

SoundExchange collects royalties for noninteractive webcasts (that is, music streams that don't allow listeners to choose songs), for satellite radio, and for music stations delivered by cable TV. Sound recording licenses for sites that stream songs on demand are administered by the PROs, not by SoundExchange.

Wondering if any digital plays have been logged for your music? Search the databases on soundexchange.com. Even if nothing pops up, it's just smart to register if you're playing on commercially released recordings. Registering with SoundExchange is free and relatively painless. Don't expect a windfall, but you may find a little cash coming your way eventually. And as CD and download sales decline, digital plays become increasingly important to anyone looking to sustain a music career.

> We're moving into an era where the compensation streams are probably going to come from several different directions, and the more you can get a baseline knowledge or understanding, the better off you're going to be. You'll at least know where you theoretically should be getting paid, which is a great place to start.
>
> —Casey Rae

SURVIVING AND THRIVING IN THE DIY AGE

Throughout these pages we've talked about the opportunities and challenges of taking the music, and the business behind it, into your own hands—from writing and performing your own songs and being your own song editor to booking yourself and producing, releasing, and promoting your own records. As the boss and chief labor force of your own cottage industry, you will find that the list of additional jobs you might take on keeps going: publicist, publisher, webmaster, manager, roadie, sound crew, merchandiser . . . Many artists shoulder all these roles out of necessity rather than choice, yet there is an appealing kind of purity about music that is written, played, and presented by a single hand. There is no filter between the creator and the listener.

The conceptual appeal of DIY doesn't change the fact that it is very tough to manage all of these tasks yourself while creating the music. You didn't become a singer-songwriter to fulfill your dream of being a mailing-list administrator or a virtuoso social-media marketer. You might find it interesting and challenging to learn everything there is to know about mechanical licensing or CMYK versus RGB color models, but there's always the danger that all this business and technical detail will steal too much attention away from the songs. If the day-to-day operation of DIY, Inc., starts to overshadow the art, what's the point of running the company in the first place? As Ani DiFranco once wrote in an open letter to the editors of *Ms.* magazine, "If I drop dead tomorrow, tell me my gravestone won't read: ani d. / CEO. Please let it read: songwriter / music maker / storyteller / freak."

Cultivating your creative life while attending to your career is a big challenge and a preoccupation of all independent artists. Let's close this tour of the singer-songwriter world with some reflections on how to maintain that elusive balance between making the music and making a living.

LOOK ON THE BRIGHT SIDE. When you're feeling bogged down by needing to raise funds for another recording project or sending out albums to reviewers who might never spin them—this is a good time to play a little game called Consider the Alternative. Every job has its tedious, annoying, or unsatisfying aspects; at least you are trying to facilitate something deeply gratifying and meaningful rather than devoting yourself to selling widgets. There really are worse things you could be doing with your time (just browse the job classifieds if you need a reminder).

> You can't play guitar all day long—you get tendinitis. You've got to do something else. If you spend a lot of time on the phone or mailing things— the business part of it—when it's time to play music, it's real fresh.
>
> —HARVEY REID

SCHEDULE YOURSELF. When you're juggling so many jobs, it can feel overwhelming if you're thinking about all of them all the time. As a way to reduce stress and improve your focus, try compartmentalizing your days more, so that you have certain hours set aside for business and for writing and, of course, your personal life. Here are a few examples of daily schedules that singer-songwriters have shared with me.

> When I'm home, I preserve my mornings for creative/reflective time, and my evenings for my friends and family. So my business hours (email, booking/ promotion, social media) are between about noon and 5 P.M., give or take.
>
> —CARSIE BLANTON

> I wake up at 4 A.M and write until 6:30 A.M. If I'm home, I pick my son up from school and hang with my family until bedtime. The time left is flexible for business/personal goals. The morning writing time and evening family time are non-negotiable.
>
> —JONATHAN BYRD

LEARN TO DELEGATE. As has been suggested numerous times in this book, for many of the jobs that need to be done, you are better off knuckling down and doing them yourself—like booking your gigs when you're starting out or releasing your first album. But you can go too far with self-reliance and drive yourself batty. So make it your mission to learn not only how to do things yourself but how to delegate—and then to refrain from micromanaging your helpers, which is both annoying to them and extra work for you. Beware the control-freak syndrome, in which you reluctantly pass a job along to someone else, constantly look over his shoulder and "correct" what he is doing, and then decide (with secret satisfaction) that since you just *have* to supervise so closely to make sure he's doing it right, you're better off just doing it yourself. There are some jobs that nobody else can do as well as you can (like writing *your* songs!), but the world is full of smart and capable people. Find them and hire them.

> *A mistake I made when I was just starting out was to try to do everything myself. While I am certainly a better businesswoman for understanding how the industry works, I neglected my creative life in the process. You have to have help—so find some good help and trust them. You can't ever completely check out of the business side of your career (which I have also done at times to devastating effect), but you can definitely find a way to supervise without devoting all your time to it.*
>
> —ERIN MCKEOWN

ENLIST YOUR FANS. Not all your help has to be paid help. Your fan base—however humble—is a pool of potential volunteers. People who discover and love the music of an emerging independent artist are particularly passionate and loyal—they feel like they have a stake in your success. Encourage them to get involved and you'll both be happy and rewarded.

> *Some people feel that you have to have that kind of curtain between the audience and the musician, but I've never felt that. One time someone asked me if I had any stalkers, and I jokingly said yeah—and I put them to work. They're not really stalkers, but big fans. I've had people come and*

sell merch for me. There's one girl that I'm going to have help with one of my websites—great.

—JILL SOBULE

You do need to be careful about assigning significant responsibilities to well-meaning but inexperienced volunteers. As mentioned in the discussion of booking, it's probably not a good idea to ask someone like this to be

JILL SOBULE

your main contact with venues, but he or she might be able to help gather information so you can follow up. Publicity involves compiling lists, doing mailings, and following up in an organized fashion—tasks you can train someone else to do. And who better to promote your virtues than a diehard fan?

Many artists effectively recruit street teams who help promote a new record or concert in their city. In return for show tickets or T-shirts or other perks, the fans put up posters, contact local radio and press, and round up people to go to a show. These relationships are invaluable and help to compensate for an independent musician's lack of marketing resources.

Think creatively about what fans might be able to do for you, and—especially—what they would enjoy doing. Ask email list subscribers and social media followers if they're interested in hosting a house concert, for instance, and then help prospective hosts figure out how to do one.

CONSIDER CROWD FUNDING. Many independent artists these days are turning to fans to help finance recordings and other projects, by running crowd-funding campaigns where people can preorder an album or give larger pledges in return for an array of rewards—from T-shirts to lessons to customized recordings and house concerts. Though many artists are initially hesitant to ask for money like this, they are often surprised how much people appreciate the opportunity to support the creation and propagation of music they love. Peter Mulvey described his decision to run his first crowd-funding campaign.

> *I felt I had a really solid record and wanted to give it the best shake possible. I felt the time was right to at least try to galvanize my fans, hire some first-rate publicity, and see how far up the flagpoles of the world I could fly this little flag. Being Midwestern, I felt a little funny asking people to pledge, but quickly became overwhelmed at the outpouring of both pledges and written expressions of enthusiastic support.*
> —PETER MULVEY

My own first crowd-funding campaign, for an album release, was thrilling and successful but also exhausting. Be aware that this is a major undertaking at every stage: budgeting the project and setting your goal, choosing and writing up your rewards, making a video, asking (and asking and asking and asking) people to pledge and share, and then fulfilling all the rewards after the campaign is over. The whole process is stressful, too, especially if you're running an all-or-nothing campaign where you have to hit your goal to receive any funds. But the benefits for a DIY artist are huge—not just because you can release your project into the world without going into huge debt, but because you've done a lot to spread your new music around, and you've deepened your relationships with your backers.

Here are a few tips for running a successful campaign.

- Be concise. People's attention spans are very short for reading project descriptions or watching videos online.
- Be specific. Say exactly what you're going to do and when, post a project budget, and be realistic.
- Be yourself, and share your passion for the music.
- Be ready to ask for help, and show your gratitude.
- Be careful not to overpromise. Rewards take time and money to deliver, so be sure to factor those costs into your funding plan.

CALL A SPECIALIST.   Aside from the ever-present clerical and grunt work, some aspects of the music business require a great deal of training and brain cells to master. Hiring a specialist can give you both peace of mind and precious time to do something else. You can have an entertainment lawyer, for instance, vet a contract for you and explain what all that impenetrable jargon means (just make sure you keep a lid on the billable hours!). Not only will that get you a more favorable contract, but the lawyer spares you having to be the hardball negotiator with people (like agents or managers) you want to treat as your friends and allies. Another example is music publishing: you can own your songs but sign with a company for publishing administration, which can become dauntingly complex when it comes to collaboration, licensing for film and TV, and international business.

If you think you can pull it off, and you want to spend your day chasing after money in Switzerland on a record that you had a song on, well then, great. But if you can get somebody for 10 percent of what you are making to do that for you, I think it's well worth it. Go write another song—that's how I look at it.

—STEVE SESKIN

BE YOURSELF. In this era, working as an independent artist means being in continual, direct contact with your audience through social media, in person, and by any means you can. Part of that communication is, by necessity, promoting your own products and projects—shows, records, workshops, funding campaigns, and so on. Yet many artists are uncomfortable in marketing/publicity mode; it makes them feel like, well, marketers or publicists rather than artists.

The way to avoid feeling like a marketer or publicist is not to act or sound like one. In reality, you are much better off anyway being an artist, and being yourself. Everyone is bombarded by slick marketing all the time. What stands out in the midst of the noise, hype, and demographic targeting is speaking to your audience (by social media or email newsletter or whatever medium) like a real person and sharing your passions—and not just for your own music.

Share, share, share. I give away videos and live recordings. I show people what the green room looks like. I post guitar lessons to my most requested songs. I share the work of other artists who turn me on. I tell stories. Every now and then I ask for something.

I'm also very proud of my work. It's worth more than I ask for. If you believe in something, you don't have to have any sales techniques. Real enthusiasm is contagious.

—JONATHAN BYRD

I try to speak from a place of genuine emotion: if I'm excited, I say that I'm excited. If I'm nervous, I say that I'm nervous. I try to avoid tropes like "Can't wait for the show on Saturday!" because I think people can detect the phoniness in that statement. Instead, I might say something like "What's really exciting about this weekend is that I'm going to play a show with the Wood Brothers, who are as sweet as they are handsome and twice as talented. Plus, currywurst!"

I find that in writing for social media (just like in songwriting), authenticity, humor, and specificity are what people respond to. When I can find the place where writing for social media feels like a creative act, I really enjoy it. And I think the fans know the difference.

—CARSIE BLANTON

SEPARATE THE PACKAGING FROM THE CREATING.   A perennial issue for songwriters is how to categorize the music they make. All manner of sounds, styles, and ideas are swirling around in the air, and each writer takes a little from here and a little from there to create something new and, in essence, uncategorizable. But the marketplace requires that music be labeled in some way, so it fits into a category in a music store or a format at the radio station or a particular type of performance venue. And that categorizing may have as much to do with how you dress and where you come from as what the songs sound like. Guitar-toting troubadours, for instance, are typically put in the folk bin regardless of what their influences and intentions are.

It's a marketing game, and you have to play it somehow if you are going to try to sell records and play gigs. So, as we noted earlier in the book, find a simple and catchy way to label your music. But don't let the barriers between styles and genres dictate the kind of music you make.

There are creative barriers and mechanical (or business) barriers. As an artist, you have direct control over only one of those: your interior creative life. At some point or another, thinking about your own art in terms of genre and definition—as "pop/rock" or "folk"—puts up as many walls for yourself as you would hope to break down. I try to make the music that makes me happiest, without regard to genre or reception. I think an important part of maturing as an independent artist is to understand what you can change and what you can't, what is your responsibility and what isn't. It is your responsibility to make the music you feel strongest about; it isn't your responsibility to label or define it. This is not to say there isn't a reason people talk about "folk" or "pop/rock"—you have to have some way of talking about music. But I like to keep that separate from the impulse to create music.

I also believe that audiences are way smarter than they are given credit for by the people who create the mechanical barriers between genres of music. People like good music, no matter if it's played on an

acoustic guitar or comes from a bin labeled "rock." I see the answer as,
"I didn't put the barrier there, neither did this audience, so together we
are going to ignore it." You have to acknowledge these barriers (get your
record in as many bins as possible!), but at the end of the day you have to
continue your creative life without regard to them.

—Erin McKeown

FIND A CREATIVE REFUGE.   Any artistic endeavor feels different once it is also (in full or in part) your livelihood. Everyone needs to preserve that feeling of creating just for the sake of creating, which is the wellspring of all great art. So make sure you get together with pals for jam sessions that have no professional purpose. Write an embarrassing song that you'd never play in public. And, perhaps, cultivate an artistic interest outside of music.

I'm painting and drawing a lot, writing stories. I don't know, it all seems
to feed each other and balance each other. Music and songs and touring
and records—I love it; I can't imagine a better job in the world, but at the
same time, it's a job and sometimes it feels like one when you are driving
five hundred miles a day and stopping at the radio station and going to
the record store and doing the gig. So it's nice to have these other things
that nobody knows much about. I really don't have to think about what
anybody thinks about it. It's refreshing. It's like when I was fifteen writing
songs—it feels like that.

—Dan Bern

THINK, THEN ACT.   As you navigate through the business, it's laudable to be independent-minded and suspicious of surrendering too much control of your music. But don't let that independent streak keep you from ever signing your name on the dotted line. Entering a business deal doesn't have to mean that you're selling out. You can preserve the integrity of what is most important—your songs—while working with other people to broaden the audience for what you do.

It's always possible (or even likely) that a relationship with a label or manager or agent won't deliver everything that you hoped for, but one of the ways you learn is by doing. Trust your gut instincts, keep your eyes open, and be especially careful when it comes to long-term agreements that you might regret in perpetuity. But when it looks and feels right, go for it. If you forever sit in your bedroom and grouse about how corrupt the music business is, your songs will never have the chance to get out in the world and make friends.

> *All business is not bad. A lot of people, and rightly so, go into the music business thinking they're going to get screwed. That's a healthy attitude to have, because then you're skeptical about anything that anybody puts in front of you, and that's what you should be. You should realize, though, that it's a sliding scale: skepticism does not necessarily equate into refusal to do a deal every time. Find out if it's a good business deal, and if it is, go for it, and hopefully you two are happy, you and the company you signed with.*
>
> —KYLE STAGGS

GET REAL (BUT NOT TOO REAL).   Having a business partner not only gives you fewer balls to juggle all the time, but it shields you from some of the day-to-day frustrations of this line of work. In every music career there's a long line of unreturned calls, rejections, and dealings with people who are insensitive, indifferent, or abrasive. This isn't personal, but it feels like it is when your songs are on the line. So having someone else out there in the trenches on your behalf can help keep your spirits up and your eyes on the prize of making the best music you can.

> *For every song that my publisher gets cut, I'm going to go out on a limb and say that there are probably 100 or 150 songs she has played for somebody to get that one. Well, first of all, I don't want to deal with all that rejection of my own songs, day after day after day. She doesn't call me and say, "Hey, I played thirty of your songs for people today, and they passed on all of them." She just calls me about the one that they took. I guess what I'm trying to say is that we need to protect ourselves a little bit as creative souls, because our emotional state is wrapped up in some of this. I think it's healthy to know what's going on in the business, but if you become consumed by it, it's bound to affect your creative process in a negative way.*
>
> —STEVE SESKIN

GIVE YOURSELF CREDIT.   In all areas of life, we progress by setting our sights on the things we haven't done, the places we haven't been, the sounds we haven't created yet. Keep your eye on that horizon, but pause from time to time to consider the steps that you have taken: the songs written, the emotions shared, the music played. It takes a lot of nerve to get up in front of people, play something that you wrote, and invite them to respond. And if your song actually moves some people or makes them laugh or sets their feet dancing—that is an extraordinary accomplishment. In the face of all the steep odds, intense competition, and slim rewards of doing this instead of or in addition to what's affectionately known as a real job, sometimes you need to acknowledge how far you have come.

> *When people ask me about being an independent musician, I say, "Well, do you really have to do this? Do you have no alternative? Does this fuel your most inner soul? Will you die without getting your music out there? In that case, you have to do whatever it takes."*
>
> *It's a constant search. How do you establish an identity in the market-place? How do you sustain a certain level of respect? "Oh, Jonatha's in town"—how do you establish that level of notoriety and persona? Sometimes you sit there and you think, "What the hell am I doing? I am this whiny creative mess and I suck and I'm never going to write another song and how are we going to pay the credit card this month . . ." And then you kind of realize, "Wait a minute, I have been doing something. I have been working. I've been making small strides in a good direction."*
>
> —JONATHA BROOKE

Small strides in a good direction: that sounds like an excellent motto. Small strides in a good direction, song to song to song.

Happy travels.

ACKNOWLEDGMENTS

This book is deeply connected to my work for *Acoustic Guitar* magazine over the last twenty-five years. Many of the artists' quotes come from my *Acoustic Guitar* interviews (some of which were collected in the book *Rock Troubadours*), and some material in these pages, such as the sections on chord progressions and rhyme, originated as magazine articles. I'm grateful to *Acoustic Guitar*'s publisher, David A. Lusterman, for permission to use published and unpublished excerpts from interviews during my years as the magazine's editor; and to all the *A.G.* editors over the years who helped shape and improve my work.

At the heart of *The Complete Singer-Songwriter* are the insights and advice generously offered over the years by so many musicians and sympathetic souls in the music business. So let me take a deep breath and thank: Rani Arbo, Dawn Atkinson, Jessica Baron, Dan Bern, Carsie Blanton, Billy Bragg, Patrick Brayer, Edie Brickell, David Bromberg, Jonatha Brooke, Greg Brown, Malcolm Burn, Jonathan Byrd, Andrew Calhoun (Waterbug Records), Lauren Calista (Rounder Records), Brandi Carlile, Rosanne Cash, Beth Nielsen Chapman, Shawn Colvin, Elvis Costello, Rodney Crowell, Catie Curtis, Alana Davis, Ani DiFranco, Iris DeMent, Jerry Douglas, Jakob Dylan, Stephen Fearing, Bob Feldman (Red House Records), Ferron, Holly Figueroa, Jim Fleming (Fleming and Associates), Nancy Fly and Seymour Guenther (Nancy Fly Agency), John Fogerty, Rhiannon Giddens, Taylor Goldsmith, José González, Mike Gordon, David Grisman, Arlo Guthrie, Phil Hanseroth, Tim Hanseroth, Ben Harbert, Ben Harper, Don Henley, Chrissie Hynde, Jewel, Ken Irwin (Rounder Records), Kathy Kallick, Lucy Kaplansky, John Keane, Brandon Kessler, Jennifer Kimball, Leo Kottke, Valerie June, Patty Larkin, G. Love, Laura Love, Griff Luneberg,

Steve Martin, John Mayer, John McCrae, Erin McKeown, Anaïs Mitchell, Joni Mitchell, Gurf Morlix, Jason Mraz, Peter Mulvey, Scott Nygaard, Tim O'Brien, Jim Olsen (Signature Sounds), Steven Page, Kenneth Pattengale, Ellis Paul, Kelly Joe Phelps, Glen Phillips, Woody Pines, Casey Rae (Future of Music Coalition), Amy Ray, Harvey Reid, Tim Reynolds, Ed Robertson, Wayne Rooks (Serling, Rooks, and Ferrara), Sean Rowe, Joey Ryan, Emily Saliers, Dylan Schorer, Darrell Scott, John Sebastian, Alynda Lee Segarra, Steve Seskin, Duncan Sheik, Paul Simon, Derek Sivers, Chris Smither, Fran Snyder, Jill Sobule, Simone Solondz, Kyle Staggs, Walkin' Jim Stoltz, Craig Street, James Taylor, Louise Taylor, Chris Thile, Richard Thompson, KT Tunstall, KC Turner, Jeff Tweedy, Suzanne Vega, Loudon Wainwright III, Sara Watkins, Sean Watkins, David Wax, Bob Weir, David Wilcox, Dar Williams, Keller Williams, Randall Wixen, and Natalia Zukerman.

As I complete the second edition, a dozen years after the publication of the first, it's poignant to realize that some of the great voices heard in these pages are no longer with us. I feel privileged to have had the chance to meet Jerry Garcia, Richie Havens, Michael Hedges, Chris Whitley, Utah Phillips, and Pete Seeger.

Many thanks to John Cerullo, Bernadette Malavarca, and everyone at Backbeat Books and Hal Leonard for the opportunity to publish this expanded second edition; to Wendy for the encouragement, feedback, companionship, and harmonies; and to Lila and Jasper, who have been busy growing up during the lifespan of this book.

ABOUT THE AUTHOR

Jeffrey Pepper Rodgers has combined his twin passions for words and music since he was a teenager. A grand-prize winner in the John Lennon Songwriting Contest, Rodgers performs original folk rock and has released five solo albums on his own Words and Music label, plus a series of videos for Homespun Music Instruction teaching his acoustic arrangements of Grateful Dead songs.

Based in upstate New York, Rodgers has performed widely both solo and with his acoustic band, including the Emerging Artist Showcase at the Falcon Ridge Folk Festival. He has collaborated onstage and in the studio with fiddler/singer-songwriter Rani Arbo, and he's shared the stage with such artists as Peter Case, Karen Savoca and Pete Heitzman, Eric Bibb, Cheryl Wheeler, Peter Mulvey, Jeffrey Foucault, Christine Lavin, and Maura Kennedy.

Rodgers is also the founding editor of *Acoustic Guitar* magazine and covers the music scene for NPR's *All Things Considered*. He is the author of *Rock Troubadours* (featuring his interviews with such artists as Jerry Garcia, Paul Simon, Joni Mitchell, and Dave Matthews), *Teach Yourself Guitar Basics* (Stringletter), and the multimedia guide *Songwriting Basics for Guitarists* (Stringletter). Rodgers teaches courses on songwriting and creative nonfiction writing in the honors program at Syracuse University and leads workshops on guitar and songwriting.

Find more on Rodgers's music and writings at jeffreypepperrodgers.com, and visit this book's companion website at completesingersongwriter.com.

PHOTO CREDITS

Brandi Carlile: Jason Merritt/Getty Images; Paul Simon: Rob Verhorst/ Getty Images; Jerry Garcia: © Rob Cohn/Photofest; James Taylor: Kevin Mazur/Getty Imags; Ben Harper: FilmMagic/Getty Images; Anais Mitchell: Matt Cowan/Getty Images; John Mayer: Getty Images; Elvis Costello: Neil H. Kitson/Getty Images; Jason Mraz: Chiaki Nozu/Getty Images; Dar Williams: Fernando Leon/Getty Images; Jeff Tweedy: Chris McKay/Getty Images; Loudon Wainwright III: Chris Felver/Getty Images; Jewel: Photofest; Indigo Girls: Gregory Rec/Getty Images; Ani DiFranco: Jay Hickerson; Suzanne Vega: Sergey Kiselev/Kimmersant Photo/Getty Images; Rodney Crowell: Ebet Roberts/Getty Imags; Joey Ryan: Getty Images; Dan Bern: Getty Images; Jill Sobule: Getty Images

INDEX